W9-ARN-676

How to use this book

A Pocket Style Manual is a quick reference for writers and researchers. As a writer, you can turn to it for advice on revising sentences for clarity, grammar, punctuation, and mechanics. As a researcher, you can refer to its documentation models and to its guidelines on citing and integrating sources. Three commonly used documentation styles are included: MLA, APA, and footnotes or endnotes.

To find information, either consult the brief table of contents inside the front cover or turn to the index at the back of the book. For many topics, the brief table of contents will send you very close to the information you're looking for (because most sections in the book are quite short). Once you have turned to a particular section, you'll find that the book's many headings help you scan for the exact advice you need.

At times you will want to consult the index. For example, you may not know from the table of contents that the issue of *is* versus *are* appears in section 10 (Make subjects and verbs agree). In that case, simply look up "*is* versus *are*" in the index. The index is also a useful way to find information in the book's longer sections, such as section 27 on MLA documentation style. Look up "MLA style" in the index, and you will find an alphabetical listing of the section's parts.

The glossaries in *A Pocket Style Manual* deserve special mention. When in doubt about the correct use of a particular word (such as *affect* and *effect*, *among* and *between*, or *hopefully*), consult section 31, a glossary of usage. When you don't understand the meaning of a grammatical term used elsewhere in the book, consult section 32, a glossary of grammatical terms. There you will find brief definitions of terms such as *adjective*, *subject*, *subordinate clause*, and *participial phrase*.

A Pocket Style Manual is meant to be consulted as the need arises. Keep it on your desk—right next to your dictionary—or tuck it into your backpack or jacket pocket and carry it with you as a ready resource.

A POCKET STYLE MANUAL

Diana Hacker

Clarity

Grammar

Punctuation and Mechanics

Documentation

Usage

Grammatical Terms

Bedford Books *of* St. Martin's Press
Boston

Note: *A Pocket Style Manual* is adapted from Diana Hacker's *A Writer's Reference*, Second Edition, and *The Bedford Handbook for Writers*, Fourth Edition.

FOR BEDFORD BOOKS

Publisher: Charles H. Christensen
Associate Publisher/General Manager: Joan E. Feinberg
Managing and Production Editor: Elizabeth M. Schaaf
Developmental Editor: Katherine A. Retan
Copyeditor: Barbara G. Flanagan
Text Design: Claire Seng-Niemoeller
Cover Design: Hannus Design Associates

Library of Congress Catalog Card Number: 92–72224

For information, write: St. Martin's Press, Inc.
175 Fifth Avenue, New York, NY 10010

Editorial Offices: Bedford Books *of* St. Martin's Press
29 Winchester Street, Boston, MA 02116

ISBN: 0–312–11494–X

CLARITY

Clarity

1. Tighten wordy sentences.

Long sentences are not necessarily wordy, nor are short sentences always concise. A sentence is wordy if its meaning can be gracefully conveyed in fewer words.

1a. Redundancies

Redundancies such as *cooperate together*, *close proximity*, *basic essentials*, and *true fact* are a common source of wordiness. There is no need to say the same thing twice.

▶ Slaves were ~~portrayed or~~ stereotyped as lazy even

  though they were the main labor force of the South.

Modifiers are redundant when their meanings are suggested by other words in the sentence.

▶ Sylvia ~~very hurriedly~~ scribbled her name and phone

  number on the back of a greasy napkin.

1b. Empty or inflated phrases

An empty word or phrase can be cut with little or no loss of meaning. An inflated phrase can be reduced to a word or two.

▶ ~~The town of~~ New Harmony, ~~located in~~ Indiana, was

  founded as a utopian community.

▶ We will file the appropriate papers ~~in the event that~~ *if*

  we are unable to meet the deadline.

INFLATED	CONCISE
along the lines of	like
at the present time	now, currently
because of the fact that	because
by means of	by
due to the fact that	because
for the purpose of	for

INFLATED	CONCISE
for the reason that	because
in order to	to
in spite of the fact that	although, though
in the event that	if
until such time as	until

1c. Needlessly complex structures

In a rough draft, sentence structures are often more complex than they need to be.

▶ ~~There is~~ *A*nother videotape ~~that~~ tells the story of

Charles Darwin and introduces the theory of evolution.

▶ ~~It is imperative that~~ *A*ll police officers *must* follow strict

procedures when apprehending a suspect.

▶ Our landlord was an elderly bachelor/ *who taught us* ~~and it was~~

~~through his guidance that we were able~~ to appreciate

country life.

2. Prefer active verbs.

As a rule, active verbs express meaning more vigorously than their duller counterparts — forms of the verb *be* or verbs in the passive voice. Forms of the verb *be* (*be, am, is, are, was, were, being,* and *been*) lack vigor because they convey no action. Passive verbs lack strength because their subjects receive the action instead of doing it.

Although forms of *be* and passive verbs have legitimate uses, if an active verb can convey your meaning as well, use it.

FORM OF *BE*	A surge of power *was* responsible for the destruction of the coolant pumps.
PASSIVE	The coolant pumps *were destroyed* by a surge of power.
ACTIVE	A surge of power *destroyed* the coolant pumps.

2a. When to replace *be* verbs

Not every *be* verb needs replacing. The forms of *be* (*be, am, is, are, was, were, being, been*) work well when you want to link a subject to a noun that clearly renames it or to a vivid adjective that describes it: Advertising *is* legalized lying. Great intellects *are* skeptical.

If a *be* verb makes a sentence needlessly wordy, however, consider replacing it. Often a phrase following the verb will contain a word (such as *destruction*) that suggests a more vigorous, active alternative (*destroyed*).

▶ Burying nuclear waste in Antarctica would ~~be in~~ *violate*

   ~~violation of~~ an international treaty.

▶ Escaping into the world of drugs, I ~~was rebellious~~ *rebelled against*

   ~~about~~ every rule set down by my parents.

2b. When to replace passive verbs

In the active voice, the subject of the sentence does the action; in the passive, the subject receives the action.

ACTIVE   The committee reached a decision.

PASSIVE   A decision was reached by the committee.

In passive sentences, the actor (in this case *committee*) frequently disappears from the sentence: A decision was reached.

In most cases, you will want to emphasize the actor, so you should use the active voice. To replace a passive verb with an active alternative, make the actor the subject of the sentence.

▶ ~~All~~ of my friends ~~were invited~~ to the party . ~~by my~~ *My mother invited all*

   ~~mother.~~

▶ As the patient undressed, scars ~~were seen~~ on her back, *the doctor saw*

   stomach, and thighs.

The passive voice is appropriate when you wish to emphasize the receiver of the action or to minimize the importance of the actor. In the following sentence, for example, the writer wished to focus on the tobacco plants, not on the people spraying them: As the time for harvest approaches, *the tobacco plants are sprayed* with a chemical to retard the growth of suckers.

3. Balance parallel ideas.

If two or more ideas are parallel, they should be expressed in parallel grammatical form.

A kiss can be a comma, a question mark, or an exclamation point. —Mistinguett

This novel is not to be tossed lightly aside, but to be hurled with great force. —Dorothy Parker

3a. Items in a series

Balance all items in a series by presenting them in parallel grammatical form.

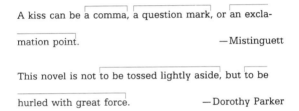

▶ Abused children commonly exhibit one or more of the following symptoms: withdrawal, rebelliousness, restlessness, and ~~they are depressed.~~ *depression.*

▶ The system has capabilities such as communicating with other computers, processing records, and *performing* mathematical functions.

3b. Paired ideas

When pairing ideas, underscore their connection by expressing them in similar grammatical form. Paired ideas are usually connected in one of three ways: (1) with a coordinating conjunction such as *and*, *but*, or *or*; (2) with a pair of correlative conjunctions such as *either . . . or*, *not only . . . but also*, or *whether . . . or*; or (3) with a word introducing a comparison, usually *than* or *as*.

▶ Many states are reducing property taxes for home-

       extending

  owners and ~~extend~~ financial aid in the form of tax

       ^

  credits to renters.

The coordinating conjunction *and* connects two verbs: *reducing . . . extending.*

▶ The shutters were not only too long but also ~~were~~ too

  wide.

The correlative conjunctions *not only . . . but also* connect two adjective phrases: *too long . . . too wide.*

                                   to ground

▶ It is easier to speak in abstractions than ~~grounding~~

                                        ^

  one's thoughts in reality.

The comparative term *than* links two infinitive phrases: *to speak . . . to ground.*

4. Add needed words.

Do not omit words necessary for grammatical or logical completeness. Readers need to see at a glance how the parts of a sentence are connected.

4a. Words in compound structures

In compound structures, words are often omitted for economy: Tom is a man who means what he says and [*who*] says what he means. Such omissions are acceptable as long as the omitted word is common to both parts of the compound structure.

If the shorter version defies grammar or idiom because an omitted word is not common to both parts of the structure, the word must be put back in.

▶ Some of the regulars are acquaintances whom we see

    who

  at work or live in our community.

    ^

The word *who* must be included because *whom live in our community* is not grammatically correct.

▶ Tribes in the South Pacific still believe *in* and live by

ancient laws.

Believe . . . by is not idiomatic English.

4b. The word *that*

Add the word *that* if there is any danger of misreading without it.

▶ Many citizens do not believe *that* the leaders of this admin-

istration are serious about reducing the deficit.

Without *that*, readers might at first think that the citizens don't believe the leaders.

4c. Words in comparisons

Comparisons should be between items that are alike. To compare unlike items is illogical and distracting.

▶ Their starting salaries are higher than *those of* other

professionals with more seniority.

Salaries must be compared with salaries, not with professionals.

5. Eliminate confusing shifts.

5a. Shifts in point of view

The point of view of a piece of writing is the perspective from which it is written: first person (*I* or *we*), second person (*you*), or third person (*he/she/it/one* or *they*). Writers who are having difficulty settling on an appropriate point of view sometimes shift confusingly from one to another. The solution is to choose a suitable perspective and then stay with it.

▶ One week our class met to practice rescuing a victim
trapped in a wrecked car. ~~You~~ *We* were graded on ~~your~~ *our*

speed and ~~your~~ *our* skill.

Shifts from the third-person singular to the third-person plural are especially common.

▶ *Police officers are*
   ~~A police officer is~~ often criticized for always being
   ∧
   there when they aren't needed and never being there

   when they are.

Although the writer might have changed *they* to *he or she* (to match the singular *officer*), the revision in the plural is more concise. See pages 27–29.

NOTE: The *I* (or *we*) point of view, which emphasizes the writer, is a good choice for writing based primarily on personal experience. The *you* point of view, which emphasizes the reader, works well for giving advice or explaining how to do something. The third-person point of view, which emphasizes the subject, is appropriate in most academic and professional writing.

5b. Shifts in tense

Consistent verb tenses clearly establish the time of the actions being described. When a passage begins in one tense and then shifts without warning and for no reason to another, readers are distracted and confused.

▶ Rescue workers put water on her face and lifted
   opened
   her head gently onto a pillow. Finally, she ~~opens~~
   ∧
   her eyes.

Writers often shift verb tenses when writing about literature. The literary convention is to describe fictional events consistently in the present tense. (See pp. 25–26.)

▶ The scarlet letter is a punishment sternly placed on
   is
   Hester's breast by the community, and yet it ~~was~~ an
   ∧
   ˙mely fanciful and imaginative product of Hester's

     ˙ework.

6. Untangle mixed constructions.

A mixed construction contains parts that do not sensibly fit together. The mismatch may be a matter of grammar or of logic.

6a. Mixed grammar

A writer should not begin with one grammatical plan and then switch without warning to another.

▶ ~~For~~ M̶ost drivers who have a blood alcohol content of

.05 percent double their risk of causing an accident.

> The phrase beginning with *For* cannot serve as the subject of the sentence. If the phrase opens the sentence, it must be followed by a subject and a verb: For most drivers who have a blood alcohol content of .05, the *risk* of causing an accident *is doubled*.

▶ Although I feel that Mr. Dawe is an excellent calculus

teacher, ~~but~~ a few minor changes in his method would

benefit both him and the class.

> The *although* clause is subordinate, so it cannot be linked to an independent clause with the coordinating conjunction *but*.

6b. Illogical connections

A sentence's subject and verb should make sense together.

▶ Under the revised plan, the elderly, *the double personal exemption for* ~~who now receive a~~

~~double personal exemption,~~ will be abolished.

> The exemption, not the elderly, will be abolished.

7. Repair misplaced and dangling modifiers.

Modifiers should point clearly to the words they modify. As a rule, related words should be kept together.

7a. Misplaced words

The most commonly misplaced words are limiting modifiers such as *only*, *even*, *almost*, *nearly*, and *just*. They should appear in front of a verb only if they modify the verb: At first I couldn't *even touch* my toes. If they limit the meaning of some other word in the sentence, they should be placed in front of that word.

▶ You will ~~only~~ need to plant one package of seeds.
     only

7b. Misplaced phrases and clauses

Although phrases and clauses can appear at some distance from the words they modify, make sure your meaning is clear. When phrases or clauses are oddly placed, absurd misreadings can result.

▶ ~~There~~ are many pictures of comedians who have
   On the walls

performed at Gavin's. ~~on the walls.~~

The comedians weren't performing on the walls; the pictures were on the walls.

▶ The robber was described as a six-foot-tall man with a
              150-pound,

mustache. ~~weighing 150 pounds.~~

The robber, not the mustache, weighed 150 pounds.

7c. Dangling modifiers

A dangling modifier fails to refer logically to any word in the sentence. Dangling modifiers are usually introductory word groups that suggest but do not name an actor. When a sentence opens with such a modifier, readers expect the subject of the following clause to name the actor. If it doesn't, the modifier dangles.

▶ ~~Opening~~ the window to let out a huge bumblebee, the
   When the driver opened

car accidentally swerved into an oncoming car.

The car didn't open the window; the driver did. The writer has revised the sentence by mentioning the driver in the opening modifier.

▶ After completing seminary training, ~~women's~~ access to

women have often been denied

the pulpit. ~~has often been denied.~~

The women (not their access to the pulpit) complete the training. The writer has revised the sentence by making *women* (not *women's access*) the subject.

7d. Split infinitives

An infinitive consists of *to* plus a verb: *to think, to dance.* When a modifier appears between its two parts, an infinitive is said to be "split": to *carefully* balance. If a split infinitive is awkward, move the modifier to another position in the sentence.

▶ The jurors were instructed to ~~very carefully~~ sift

very carefully.

through the evidence.

When a split infinitive is more natural and less awkward than alternative phrasing, most readers find it acceptable. *We decided to actually enforce the law* is a perfectly natural construction in English. *We decided actually to enforce the law* is not.

8. Provide some variety.

When a rough draft is filled with too many same-sounding sentences, try to inject some variety — as long as you can do so without sacrificing clarity or ease of reading.

8a. Combining choppy sentences

If a series of short sentences sounds choppy, consider combining some of them. Look for opportunities to tuck some of your ideas into subordinate clauses. Subordinate clauses, which contain subjects and verbs, begin with words like these: *after, although, because, before, if, since, that, unless, until, when, where, which,* and *who.*

▶ The losing team was made up of superstars. ~~They~~

who

acted as isolated individuals on the court.

▶ *Because*
Jean had helped John through school./ ~~He~~ *he* decided to

do the same for her.

Also look for opportunities to tuck some of your ideas into phrases, word groups that lack subjects or verbs (or both).

▶ Karate~~,~~ ~~is~~ a discipline based on the philosophy of

nonviolence./ ~~It~~ teaches the art of self-defense.

▶ *Noticing*   *James*
~~James noticed~~ that the sky was glowing orange,/ ~~He~~

bent down to crawl into the bunker.

At times it will make sense to combine short sentences by joining them with *and*, *but*, or *or*.

▶   *and*
Shore houses were flooded up to the first floor./ Brandt's

Lighthouse was swallowed by the sea.

CAUTION: Avoid stringing a series of sentences together with *and*, *but*, or *or*. For sentence variety, place some of the ideas in subordinate clauses or phrases.

▶ *After four hours,*
~~Four hours went by, and~~ a rescue truck finally arrived,

but by that time we had been evacuated in a helicopter.

8b. Varying sentence openings

Most sentences in English begin with the subject, move to the verb, and continue to an object, with modifiers tucked in along the way or put at the end. For the most part, such sentences are fine. Put too many of them in a row, however, and they become monotonous.

Words, phrases, or clauses modifying the verb can often be inserted ahead of the subject.

▶ *Eventually a*
~~A~~ few drops of sap ~~eventually~~ began to trickle into the

pail.

Just as the sun was coming up, a

▶ ~~A~~ pair of black ducks flew over the pond, ~~just as the~~

~~sun was coming up.~~

Adjectives and participial phrases can frequently be moved to the beginning of a sentence without loss of clarity.

Dejected and withdrawn,

▶ Edward, ~~dejected and withdrawn,~~ nearly gave up his

search for a job.

A   *John and I*

▶ ~~John and I,~~ anticipating a peaceful evening, sat down

at the campfire to brew a cup of coffee.

9. Find an appropriate voice.

An appropriate voice is one that suits your subject, engages your audience, and conforms to the conventions of the genre in which you are writing. When in doubt about the conventions of a particular genre—lab reports, informal essays, business memos, and so on—take a look at models written by experts in the field.

In the academic, professional, and business worlds, three kinds of language are generally considered inappropriate: jargon, which sounds too pretentious; slang, which sounds too breezy; and sexist English, which offends many readers.

9a. Jargon

Jargon is specialized language used among members of a trade, profession, or group. Use jargon only when readers will be familiar with it; even then, use it only when plain English will not do as well.

JARGON   For many decades the indigenous body politic of South Africa attempted to negotiate legal enfranchisement without result.

REVISED   For many decades the native population of South Africa negotiated in vain for the right to vote.

Broadly defined, jargon includes puffed-up language designed more to impress readers than to inform them. Common examples in business, government, higher education, and the military are given in the following list, with plain English translations in parentheses.

commence (begin)	indicator (sign)
components (parts)	input (advice)
endeavor (try)	optimal (best)
exit (leave)	parameters (boundaries)
facilitate (help)	prior to (before)
factor (consideration, cause)	prioritize (set priorities)
finalize (finish)	utilize (use)
impact on (affect)	viable (workable)

Sentences filled with jargon are hard to read, and they are often wordy as well.

▶ If managers ~~have adequate input from~~ *listen to* their subordinates, they can ~~effectuate more viable~~ *make better* decisions.

▶ All ~~employees functioning in the capacity of~~ work-study students ~~are required to give evidence of current enrollment.~~ *must prove that they are currently enrolled.*

9b. Slang

Slang is an informal and sometimes private vocabulary that expresses the solidarity of a group such as teenagers, rock musicians, or baseball fans. Although it does have a certain vitality, slang is a code that not everyone understands, and it is too informal for most written work.

▶ The government's "filth" guidelines will ~~gross you out.~~ *disgust you.*

9c. Sexist language

Sexist language is language that stereotypes or demeans men or women, usually women. Such language arises from stereotypical thinking, from traditional pronoun use, and from words used to refer indefinitely to both sexes.

Stereotypical thinking.   In your writing, avoid referring to any one profession as exclusively male or exclusively female (such as referring to nurses in general as female). Also avoid using different conventions when identifying women and men (such as giving a woman's marital status but not a man's).

▶ All executives' ~~wives~~ *spouses* are cordially invited to the

company picnic.

▶ Jake Stein, attorney, and ~~Mrs.~~ Cynthia Jones, ~~mother~~ *graphic designer,*

~~of three,~~ are running for city council.

***The pronouns* he *and* him.** Traditionally, *he*, *him*, and *his* were used to refer indefinitely to persons of either sex: *A journalist is stimulated by his deadline.* You can avoid such usage in one of three ways: substitute a pair of pronouns (*he or she*, *his or her*); reword in the plural; or revise the sentence so the problem does not arise.

▶ A journalist is stimulated by his *or her* deadline.

▶ ~~A journalist is~~ *Journalists are* stimulated by ~~his deadline.~~ *their deadlines*

▶ A journalist is stimulated by ~~his~~ *a* deadline.

Man *words*. Like *he* and *his*, the nouns *man* and *men* and related words containing them were once used indefinitely to refer to persons of either sex. Use gender-neutral terms instead.

INAPPROPRIATE	APPROPRIATE
chairman	chairperson, chair
congressman	representative, legislator
fireman	firefighter
mailman	mail carrier, postal worker
mankind	people, humans
to man	to operate, to staff
weatherman	meteorologist, forecaster
workman	worker, laborer

GRAMMAR

Grammar

10. Make subjects and verbs agree.

In the present tense, verbs agree with their subjects in number (singular or plural) and in person (first, second, or third). The present-tense ending *-s* is used on a verb if its subject is third-person singular; otherwise the verb takes no ending. Consider, for example, the present-tense forms of the verb *give*:

	SINGULAR	PLURAL
FIRST PERSON	I give	we give
SECOND PERSON	you give	you give
THIRD PERSON	he/she/it gives	they give
	Alison gives	parents give

The verb *be* varies from this pattern, and unlike any other verb it has special forms in *both* the present and the past tense.

PRESENT-TENSE FORMS OF *BE*		PAST-TENSE FORMS OF *BE*	
I am	we are	I was	we were
you are	you are	you were	you were
he/she/it is	they are	he/she/it was	they were

Problems with subject-verb agreement tend to arise in certain tricky contexts, which are detailed in this section.

10a. Words between subject and verb

Word groups often come between the subject and the verb. Such word groups, usually modifying the subject, may contain a noun that at first appears to be the subject. By mentally stripping away such modifiers, you can isolate the noun that is in fact the subject.

The *tulips* in the pot on the balcony *need* watering.

▶ High levels of air pollution ~~causes~~ *Cause* damage to the respiratory tract.

The subject is *levels*, not *pollution*.

▶ A good set of golf clubs <u>cost</u> about eight hundred
    costs
    ∧

dollars.

The subject is *set*, not *clubs*.

NOTE: Phrases beginning with the prepositions *as well as*, *in addition to*, *accompanied by*, *together with*, and *along with* do not make a singular subject plural: My sister, accompanied by her husband, *was* [not *were*] seated at the head table.

10b. Subjects joined by *and*

Compound subjects joined by *and* are nearly always plural.

▶ Jill's natural ability and her desire to help others <u>has</u>
                                                have
                                                 ∧

led to a career in the ministry.

If the parts of the subject form a single unit, however, you may treat the subject as singular: Bacon and eggs *is* my favorite breakfast.

10c. Subjects joined by *or* or *nor*

With compound subjects connected by *or* or *nor*, make the verb agree with the part of the subject nearer to the verb.

▶ If a relative or neighbor <u>are</u> abusing a child, notify the
                            is
                             ∧

police.

▶ Neither my cousin nor his rowdy friends <u>was</u> accused
                                      were
                                           ∧

of the prank.

10d. Indefinite pronouns such as *someone*

Indefinite pronouns refer to nonspecific persons or things. Even though the following indefinite pronouns may seem to have plural meanings, treat them as singular in formal English: *anybody, anyone, each, either, everybody, everyone, everything, neither, none, no one, somebody, someone, something.*

▶ Nearly everyone on the panel ~~favor~~ *favors* the arms control

  agreement.

▶ Each of the furrows ~~have~~ *has* been seeded.

A few indefinite pronouns (*all*, *any*, *some*) may be singular or plural depending on the noun or pronoun they refer to: *Some* of the *lemonade has* disappeared. *Some* of the *rocks were* slippery.

10e. Collective nouns such as *jury*

Collective nouns such as *jury, committee, club, audience, crowd, class, troop, family*, and *couple* name a class or a group. In American English collective nouns are usually treated as singular: They emphasize the group as a unit.

▶ The scout troop ~~meet~~ *meets* in our basement on Tuesdays.

Occasionally, when there is some reason to draw attention to the individual members of the group, a collective noun may be treated as plural: A young couple *were* arguing about politics while holding hands. (Only individuals can argue and hold hands.)

NOTE: When units of measurement are used collectively, treat them as singular: Three-fourths of the pie has been eaten. When they refer to individual persons or things, treat them as plural: One-fourth of the children were sick.

10f. Subject after verb

Verbs ordinarily follow subjects. When this normal order is reversed, it is easy to become confused.

▶ At the back of the room ~~is~~ *are* a small aquarium and an

  enormous terrarium.

   The subject *aquarium and terrarium* is plural.

The subject always follows the verb in sentences beginning with *there is* or *there are* (or *there was* or *there were*).

▶ There ~~was~~ a social worker and a crew of twenty
                                 were
  volunteers.

  The subject *worker and crew* is plural.

10g. *Who*, *which*, and *that*

Like most pronouns, the relative pronouns *who*, *which*,
and *that* have antecedents, nouns or pronouns to which
they refer. Relative pronouns used as subjects take verbs
that agree with their antecedents.

  Take a suit that travels well.

  Problems arise with the constructions *one of the* and
only one of the. As a rule, treat *one of the* constructions
as plural, *only one of the* constructions as singular.

▶ Our ability to use language is one of the things that
  ~~sets~~ us apart from animals.
  set

  The antecedent of *that* is *things*, not *one.* Several things set
  us apart from animals.

▶ Dr. Barker knew that Frank was the only one of his
  sons who ~~were~~ responsible enough to handle the
         was
  estate.

  The antecedent of *who* is *one*, not *sons.* Only one son was
  responsible enough.

10h. Plural form, singular meaning

Words such as *athletics, economics, mathematics, physics,
statistics, measles,* and *news* are usually singular, despite
their plural form.

▶ Statistics ~~are~~ among the most difficult courses in our
           is
  program.

EXCEPTION: When they describe separate items rather
than a collective body of knowledge, words such as *ath-*

letics, *mathematics*, and *statistics* are plural: The *statistics* on school retention rates *are* impressive.

10i. Titles and words mentioned as words

Titles and words mentioned as words are singular.

▶ *Lost Cities* ~~describe~~ *describes* the discoveries of many ancient

civilizations.

▶ *Controlled substances* ~~are~~ *is* a euphemism for illegal

drugs.

11. Be alert to other problems with verbs.

The verb is the heart of the sentence, so it is important to get it right. Section 10 deals with the problem of subject-verb agreement. This section describes a few other potential problems with verbs.

11a. Irregular verbs

For all regular verbs, the past-tense and past-participle forms are the same, ending in -*ed* or -*d*, so there is no danger of confusion. This is not true, however, for irregular verbs such as the following.

BASE FORM	PAST TENSE	PAST PARTICIPLE
begin	began	begun
fly	flew	flown
ride	rode	ridden

The past-tense form, which never has a helping verb, expresses action that occurred entirely in the past. The past participle is used with a helping verb — either with *has*, *have*, or *had* to form one of the perfect tenses or with *be*, *am*, *is*, *are*, *was*, *were*, *being*, or *been* to form the passive voice.

PAST TENSE	Last July, we *went* to Paris.
PAST PARTICIPLE	We have *gone* to Paris twice.

When you aren't sure which verb form to choose (*went* or *gone*, *began* or *begun*, and so on), consult the list below. Choose the past tense form if your sentence doesn't have a helping verb; choose the past participle form if it does.

▶ Yesterday we ~~seen~~ *saw* an unidentified flying object.

Because there is no helping verb, the past-tense form *saw* is required.

▶ The driver had apparently ~~fell~~ *fallen* asleep at the wheel.

Because of the helping verb *had*, the past-participle form *fallen* is required.

Common irregular verbs

BASE FORM	PAST TENSE	PAST PARTICIPLE
arise	arose	arisen
awake	awoke, awaked	awaked, awoke
be	was, were	been
beat	beat	beaten, beat
become	became	become
begin	began	begun
bend	bent	bent
bite	bit	bitten, bit
blow	blew	blown
break	broke	broken
bring	brought	brought
build	built	built
burst	burst	burst
buy	bought	bought
catch	caught	caught
choose	chose	chosen
cling	clung	clung
come	came	come
cost	cost	cost
deal	dealt	dealt
dig	dug	dug
dive	dived, dove	dived
do	did	done
drag	dragged	dragged
draw	drew	drawn
dream	dreamed, dreamt	dreamed, dreamt
drink	drank	drunk
drive	drove	driven
eat	ate	eaten

BASE FORM	PAST TENSE	PAST PARTICIPLE
fall	fell	fallen
fight	fought	fought
find	found	found
fly	flew	flown
forget	forgot	forgotten, forgot
freeze	froze	frozen
get	got	gotten, got
give	gave	given
go	went	gone
grow	grew	grown
hang (suspend)	hung	hung
hang (execute)	hanged	hanged
have	had	had
hear	heard	heard
hide	hid	hidden
hurt	hurt	hurt
keep	kept	kept
know	knew	known
lay (put)	laid	laid
lead	led	led
lend	lent	lent
let (allow)	let	let
lie (recline)	lay	lain
lose	lost	lost
make	made	made
prove	proved	proved, proven
read	read	read
ride	rode	ridden
ring	rang	rung
rise (get up)	rose	risen
run	ran	run
say	said	said
see	saw	seen
send	sent	sent
set (place)	set	set
shake	shook	shaken
shoot	shot	shot
shrink	shrank	shrunk, shrunken
sing	sang	sung
sink	sank	sunk
sit (be seated)	sat	sat
slay	slew	slain
sleep	slept	slept
speak	spoke	spoken
spin	spun	spun
spring	sprang	sprung

BASE FORM	PAST TENSE	PAST PARTICIPLE
stand	stood	stood
steal	stole	stolen
sting	stung	stung
strike	struck	struck, stricken
swear	swore	sworn
swim	swam	swum
swing	swung	swung
take	took	taken
teach	taught	taught
throw	threw	thrown
wake	woke, waked	waked, woken
wear	wore	worn
wring	wrung	wrung
write	wrote	written

11b. Tense

Tenses indicate the time of an action in relation to the time of the speaking or writing about that action. The most common problem with tenses — shifting from one tense to another — is discussed on page 8. Other problems with tenses are detailed in this section, after the following survey of tenses.

Survey of tenses.   Tenses are classified as present, past, and future, with simple, perfect, and progressive forms for each.

The simple tenses indicate relatively simple time relations. The present tense is used primarily for actions occurring at the time of the speaking or for actions occurring regularly. The past tense is used for actions completed in the past. The future tense is used for actions that will occur in the future. In the following table, the simple tenses are given for the regular verb *walk*, the irregular verb *ride*, and the highly irregular verb *be*.

PRESENT TENSE

SINGULAR		PLURAL	
I	walk, ride, am	we	walk, ride, are
you	walk, ride, are	you	walk, ride, are
he/she/it	walks, rides, is	they	walk, ride, are

PAST TENSE

SINGULAR		PLURAL	
I	walked, rode, was	we	walked, rode, were
you	walked, rode, were	you	walked, rode, were
he/she/it	walked, rode, was	they	walked, rode, were

FUTURE TENSE
I, you, he/she/it, we, they   will walk, ride, be

More complex time relations are indicated by the perfect tenses. A verb in one of the perfect tenses (a form of *have* plus the past participle) expresses an action that was or will be completed at the time of another action.

PRESENT PERFECT
I, you, we, they   have walked, ridden, been
he/she/it   has walked, ridden, been

PAST PERFECT
I, you, he/she/it, we, they   had walked, ridden, been

FUTURE PERFECT
I, you, he/she/it, we, they   will have walked, ridden, been

Each of the six tenses just mentioned has a progressive form used to express a continuing action. A progressive verb consists of a form of *be* followed by the present participle.

PRESENT PROGRESSIVE
I   am walking, riding, being
he/she/it   is walking, riding, being
you, we, they   are walking, riding, being

PAST PROGRESSIVE
I, he/she/it   was walking, riding, being
you, we, they   were walking, riding, being

FUTURE PROGRESSIVE
I, you, he/she/it, we, they   will be walking, riding, being

PRESENT PERFECT PROGRESSIVE
I, you, we, they   have been walking, riding,
                            being
he/she/it   has been walking, riding, being

PAST PERFECT PROGRESSIVE
I, you, he/she/it, we, they   had been walking, riding, being

FUTURE PERFECT PROGRESSIVE
I, you, he/she/it, we, they   will have been walking, riding,
                                being

Special uses of the present tense.   Use the present tense when writing about literature or when expressing general truths.

▶ Don Quixote, in Cervantes's novel, ~~was~~ *is* an idealist ill

     suited for life in the real world.

▶ Galileo taught that the earth ~~revolved~~ *revolves* around the sun.

The past perfect tense.   The past perfect tense is used for an action already completed by the time of another past action. This tense consists of a past participle preceded by *had* (*had worked*, *had gone*).

▶ We built our cabin forty feet above an abandoned

     quarry that ~~was~~ *had been* flooded in 1920 to create a lake.

11c. Mood

There are three moods in English: the *indicative*, used for facts, opinions, and questions; the *imperative*, used for orders or advice; and the *subjunctive*, used for wishes, conditions contrary to fact, and requests or recommendations. Of these three moods, the subjunctive is most likely to cause problems.

     Use the subjunctive mood for wishes and in *if* clauses expressing conditions contrary to fact. The subjunctive in such cases is the past tense form of the verb; in the case of *be*, it is always *were* (not *was*), even if the subject is singular.

     We wish that Janet *drove* to school every day.

     If I *were* a member of Congress, I would vote for
     the bill.

     Use the subjunctive mood in *that* clauses following verbs such as *ask*, *insist*, *recommend*, and *request*. The subjunctive in such cases is the base (or dictionary) form of the verb.

     Dr. Chung insists that her students *be* on time.

     We recommend that Dawson *file* form 1050 soon.

11d. Voice

Transitive verbs (those that can take direct objects) appear in either the active or the passive voice. In the active voice, the subject of the sentence does the action; in the passive, the subject receives the action.

ACTIVE   John *hit* the ball.

PASSIVE   The ball *was hit* by John.

Because the active voice is simpler and more direct, it is usually more appropriate than the passive. (See section 2.)

12. Use pronouns with care.

Pronouns are words that substitute for nouns: *he, it, them, her, me,* and so on. Four frequently encountered problems with pronouns are discussed in this section:

- a.   pronoun-antecedent agreement (singular vs. plural)
- b.   pronoun reference (clarity)
- c.   case of personal pronouns (such as *I* vs. *me*)
- d.   *who* vs. *whom*

12a. Pronoun-antecedent agreement

The antecedent of a pronoun is the word the pronoun refers to. A pronoun and its antecedent agree when they are both singular or both plural.

SINGULAR   The *doctor* finished *her* rounds.

PLURAL   The *doctors* finished *their* rounds.

Writers are sometimes tempted to choose the plural pronoun *they* (or *their*) to refer to a singular antecedent. The temptation is greatest when the singular antecedent is an indefinite pronoun, a generic noun, or a collective noun.

Indefinite pronouns.   Indefinite pronouns refer to non-specific persons or things. Even though some of the following indefinite pronouns may seem to have plural meanings, treat them as singular in formal English: *anybody, anyone, each, either, everybody, everyone, everything, neither, none, no one, someone, something.*

In this class *everyone* performs at *his or her* [not *their*] fitness level.

When *they* or *their* refers mistakenly to a singular antecedent such as *everyone*, you will usually have three options for revision:

1. Replace *they* with *he or she* (or *their* with *his or her*);
2. make the singular antecedent plural; or
3. rewrite the sentence.

Because the *he or she* construction is wordy, often the second or third revision strategy is more effective.

▶ When someone has been drinking, ~~they are~~ more likely
   he or she is
   to speed.

▶ When ~~someone has~~ been drinking, they are more likely
   drivers have
   to speed.

▶ ~~When someone~~ has been drinking, ~~they are~~ more likely
   Someone who   *is*
   to speed.

NOTE: The traditional use of *he* (or *his*) to refer to persons of either sex is now widely considered sexist. (See pp. 14–15.)

Generic nouns.   A generic noun represents a typical member of a group, such as *a student*, or any member of a group, such as *any musician*. Although generic nouns may seem to have plural meanings, they are singular.

   Every *runner* must train rigorously if *he or she* wants [not *they want*] to excel.

When *they* or *their* refers mistakenly to a generic noun, you will usually have the same three revision options as for indefinite pronouns.

▶ A medical student must study hard if ~~they want~~ to
   he or she wants
   succeed.

▶ A medical ~~student~~ must study hard if they want to
   Medical students
   succeed.

▶ A medical student must study hard ~~if they want~~ to

succeed.

Collective nouns.   Collective nouns such as *jury*, *committee*, *audience*, *crowd*, *family*, and *team* name a class or group. In American English, collective nouns are usually singular because they emphasize the group functioning as a unit.

> The planning *committee* granted *its* [not *their*] permission to build.

If the members of the group function individually, however, you may treat the noun as plural: The family put their signatures on the document. Or you might add a plural antecedent such as *members* to the sentence: The members of the family put their signatures on the document.

12b. Pronoun reference
A pronoun should refer clearly to its antecedent. A pronoun's reference will be unclear if it is ambiguous, implied, vague, or indefinite.

Ambiguous reference.   Ambiguous reference occurs when the pronoun could refer to two possible antecedents.

▶ When Aunt Harriet put ~~the cake~~ *it* on the table, ~~it~~ *the cake*

collapsed.

▶ Tom told James ~~, that he had~~ *, "You have* won the lottery. *"*

> What collapsed—the cake or the table? Who won the lottery—Tom or James? The revisions eliminate the ambiguity.

Implied reference.   A pronoun must refer to a specific antecedent, not to a word that is implied but not present in the sentence.

▶ After braiding Ann's hair, Sue decorated **them** *the braids* with

ribbons.

Modifiers, such as possessives, cannot serve as antecedents. A modifier merely implies the noun that the pronoun might logically refer to.

▶ In ~~Camilla's~~ *her* autobiography, ~~she~~ *Camilla* reveals the story
         ∧   ∧

  behind her short stay in prison.

Vague reference of *this, that, or* which.   The pronouns *this, that,* and *which* should not refer vaguely to earlier word groups or ideas. These pronouns should refer to specific antecedents. When a pronoun's reference is too vague, either replace the pronoun with a noun or supply an antecedent to which the pronoun clearly refers.

▶ More and more often, especially in large cities, we are

  finding ourselves victims of serious crimes. We learn to
                       our fate
  accept ~~this~~ with minor complaints.
         ∧

▶ Romeo and Juliet were both too young to have
                                 a fact
  acquired much wisdom, which accounts for their
                        ∧

  rash actions.

Indefinite reference of *they, it, or* you.   The pronoun *they* should refer to a specific antecedent. Do not use *they* to refer indefinitely to persons who have not been specifically mentioned.

▶ Sometimes a list of ways to save energy is included
                            the gas company suggests
  in the gas bill. For example, ~~they suggest~~ setting a
                               ∧

  moderate temperature for the hot water heater.

The word *it* should not be used indefinitely in constructions such as "In the article it says that. . . ."

                The
▶ ~~In the~~ encyclopedia ~~it~~ states that male moths can smell
  ∧

  female moths from several miles away.

The pronoun *you* is appropriate when the writer is addressing the reader directly: Once you have kneaded the dough, let it rise in a warm place. Except in informal contexts, however, the indefinite *you* (meaning "anyone in general") is inappropriate.

▶ In advanced chemistry ~~you~~ must work hard to earn a C.
  [*students*] [∧]

12c. Case of personal pronouns such as *I* versus *me*

The personal pronouns in the following list change what is known as case form according to their grammatical function in a sentence. Pronouns functioning as subjects or subject complements appear in the *subjective* case; those functioning as objects appear in the *objective* case; and those functioning as possessives appear in the *possessive* case.

SUBJECTIVE CASE	OBJECTIVE CASE	POSSESSIVE CASE
I	me	my
we	us	our
you	you	your
he/she/it	him/her/it	his/her/its
they	them	their

For the most part, you know how to use these forms correctly. In the following situations, however, you may have difficulty choosing between *I* and *me*, *she* and *her*, and so on.

Compound word groups. When a subject or object appears as part of a compound structure, you may occasionally become confused. To test for the correct pronoun, mentally strip away all of the compound structure except for the pronoun in question.

▶ While diving for pearls, Ikiko and ~~her~~ found a treasure
  [*she*] [∧]

chest full of gold bars.

Ikiko and she is the subject of the verb *found*. Strip away the words *Ikiko and* to test for the correct pronoun: *she found* [not *her found*].

▶ The most traumatic experience for her father and ~~I~~
  [*me*] [∧]

occurred long after her operation.

Her father and me is the object of the preposition *for*. Strip away the words *her father and* to test for the correct pronoun: *for me* [not *for I*].

Subject complements.   Use subjective-case pronouns for subject complements, which rename or describe the subject and usually follow *be*, *am*, *is*, *are*, *was*, *were*, *being*, or *been*.

▶ Sandra confessed that the artist was ~~her~~.   *she*

> If *artist was she* seems too stilted, rewrite the sentence: Sandra confessed that she was the artist.

Appositives.   Appositives, noun phrases that rename nouns or pronouns, have the same function as the words they rename. To test for the correct pronoun, mentally strip away the words that the appositive renames.

▶ The chief strategists, Dr. Bell and ~~me~~, could not agree   *I,*

on a plan.

> The appositive *Dr. Bell and I* renames the subject, *strategists*. Test: *Dr. Bell and I could not agree* [not *Dr. Bell and me could not agree*].

▶ The reporter interviewed only two witnesses, the shop-keeper and ~~I~~.   *me.*

> The appositive *the shopkeeper and me* renames the direct object, *witnesses*. Test: *interviewed the shopkeeper and me* [not *interviewed the shopkeeper and I*].

We *or* us *before a noun.*   When deciding whether *we* or *us* should precede a noun, choose the pronoun that would be appropriate if the noun were omitted.

▶ ~~Us~~ tenants would rather fight than move.   *We*

> Test: *We would rather fight* [not *Us would rather fight*].

▶ Management is short-changing ~~we~~ tenants.   *us*

> Test: *Management is short-changing us* [not *Management is short-changing we*].

Pronoun after* than *or* as.   Sentence parts, usually verbs, are often omitted in comparisons beginning with *than* or *as*. To test for the correct pronoun, finish the sentence.

▶ My husband is six years older than ~~me.~~ *I.*

Test: *than I* [am].

▶ We respected no other candidate in the election as
much as ~~she.~~ *her.*

Test: *as* [*we respected*] her.

Pronoun before or after an infinitive. An infinitive is the word *to* followed by a verb. Both subjects and objects of infinitives take the objective case.

▶ Ms. Wilson asked John and ~~I~~ *me* to drive the senator and
~~she~~ *her* to the airport.

John and me is the subject and *senator and her* is the object of the infinitive *to drive.*

Pronoun or noun before a gerund. If a pronoun modifies a gerund, use the possessive case: *my, our, your, his/her/its, their.* A gerund is a verb form ending in *-ing* that functions as a noun.

▶ My parents always tolerated ~~us~~ *our* talking after the lights
were out.

Nouns as well as pronouns may modify gerunds. To form the possessive case of a noun, use an apostrophe and an *-s* (*a victim's suffering*) or just an apostrophe (*victims' suffering*). (See pp. 59–60.)

▶ We had to pay a fifty-dollar fine for ~~Brenda~~ *Brenda's* driving
without a permit.

12d. Who *or* whom

Who, a subjective-case pronoun, can be used only for subjects and subject complements. *Whom*, an objective-case pronoun, can be used only for objects. The words *who* and *whom* appear primarily in subordinate clauses or in questions.

In subordinate clauses. When deciding whether to use *who* or *whom* in a subordinate clause, check for the word's function *within the clause*.

▶ He tells that story to ~~whomever~~ *whoever* will listen.

> *Whoever* is the subject of *will listen*. The entire subordinate clause *whoever will listen* is the object of the preposition *to*.

▶ You will work with our senior engineers, ~~who~~ *whom* you will

   meet later.

> *Whom* is the direct object of the verb *will meet*. This becomes clear if you restructure the clause: *you will meet whom later*.

In questions. When deciding whether to use *who* or *whom* in a question, check for the word's function *within the question*.

▶ ~~Whom~~ *Who* was accused of receiving Mafia funds?

> *Who* is the subject of the verb *was accused*.

▶ ~~Who~~ *Whom* did the party nominate?

> *Whom* is the direct object of the verb *did nominate*. This becomes clear if you restructure the question: *The party did nominate whom*?

13. Choose adjectives and adverbs with care.

Adjectives modify nouns or pronouns; adverbs modify verbs, adjectives, or other adverbs.

Many adverbs are formed by adding *-ly* to adjectives (*formal, formally*). But don't assume that all words ending in *-ly* are adverbs or that all adverbs end in *-ly*. Some adjectives end in *-ly* (*lovely, friendly*) and some adverbs don't (*always, here*). When in doubt, consult a dictionary.

13a. Adverbs

Use adverbs, not adjectives, to modify verbs, adjectives, and adverbs. Adverbs usually answer one of these questions: When? Where? How? Why? Under what conditions? How often? To what degree?

The incorrect use of adjectives in place of adverbs to modify verbs occurs primarily in casual or nonstandard speech.

> ▶ The arrangement worked out *perfectly* for everyone.

The incorrect use of the adjective *good* in place of the adverb *well* is especially common in casual and nonstandard speech.

> ▶ We were delighted that Nicole had done so *well* on the
>
> exam.

Adjectives are sometimes incorrectly used to modify adjectives or other adverbs.

> ▶ For a man his age, Joe plays squash *really* well.

13b. Adjectives

Adjectives ordinarily precede nouns, but they can also function as subject complements following linking verbs (usually a form of *be*: *be*, *am*, *is*, *are*, *was*, *were*, *being*, *been*). When an adjective functions as a subject complement, it describes the subject.

Justice is *blind*.

Problems can arise with verbs such as *smell*, *taste*, *look*, *appear*, *grow*, and *feel*, which may or may not be linking. If the word following one of these verbs describes the subject, use an adjective; if it modifies the verb, use an adverb.

ADJECTIVE   The detective looked *cautious*.

ADVERB   The detective looked *cautiously* for the
                fingerprints.

Linking verbs usually suggest states of being, not actions. For example, to look cautious suggests the state of being cautious, whereas to look cautiously is to perform an action in a cautious way.

▶ Some flowers smell surprisingly ~~badly.~~ *bad.*

▶ Lori looked ~~well~~ *good* in her new raincoat.

> The verbs *smell* and *looked* suggest states of being, not ac-
> tions, so they should be followed by adjectives.

13c. Comparatives and superlatives

Most adjectives and adverbs have three forms: the positive, the comparative, and the superlative.

POSITIVE	COMPARATIVE	SUPERLATIVE
soft	softer	softest
fast	faster	fastest
careful	more careful	most careful
bad	worse	worst
good	better	best

Comparative versus superlative.   Use the comparative to compare two things, the superlative to compare
three or more.

▶ Which of these two brands of toothpaste is ~~best?~~ *better?*

▶ Hobbs is the ~~more~~ *most* qualified of the three applicants.

Form of comparatives and superlatives.   To form
comparatives and superlatives of most one- and two-
syllable adjectives, use the endings *-er* and *-est*: *smooth,
smoother, smoothest*. With longer adjectives, use *more*
and *most* (or *less* and *least*): *exciting, more exciting, most
exciting*.

  Some one-syllable adverbs take the endings *-er* and
-est (*fast, faster, fastest*), but longer adverbs and all of
those ending in *-ly* use *more* and *most* (or *less* and *least*).

14. Repair sentence fragments.

As a rule, do not treat a piece of a sentence as if it were
a sentence. To be a sentence, a word group must consist
of at least one full independent clause. An independent
clause has a subject and a verb, and it either stands alone

as a sentence or could stand alone. Some fragments are clauses that contain a subject and a verb but begin with a subordinating word. Others are phrases that lack a subject, a verb, or both.

You can repair a fragment in one of two ways: Either pull the fragment into a nearby sentence, punctuating the new sentence correctly, or turn the fragment into a sentence.

14a. Fragmented clauses

A subordinate clause is patterned like a sentence, with both a subject and a verb, but it begins with a word that tells readers it cannot stand alone—a word such as *after*, *although*, *because*, *before*, *if*, *so that*, *that*, *though*, *unless*, *until*, *when*, *where*, *who*, and *which*.

Most fragmented clauses beg to be pulled into a sentence nearby.

> ▶ Jane will address the problem of limited on-campus
>
> parking. ~~If~~ *if* she is elected special student adviser.

If a fragmented clause cannot be gracefully combined with a nearby sentence, try rewriting it. The simplest way to turn a fragmented clause into a sentence is to delete the opening word or words that mark it as subordinate.

> ▶ Violence has produced much fear among teachers at
>
> Dean Junior High. ~~So that~~ *S*elf-preservation, in fact,
>
> has become their primary aim.

14b. Fragmented phrases

Like subordinate clauses, certain phrases are sometimes mistaken for sentences. Frequently a fragmented phrase may simply be attached to a nearby sentence.

> ▶ On Sundays, James read the newspaper's employment
>
> listings. ~~Scrutinizing~~ *scrutinizing* every position that looked
>
> promising.

The word group beginning with *Scrutinizing* is a verbal phrase, not a sentence.

▶ Mary is suffering from agoraphobia, A fear of the outside world.

> *A fear of the outside world* is an appositive phrase, not a
> sentence.

▶ It has been said that there are only three indigenous
American art forms: Jazz, musical comedy, and soap
operas.

> Clearly the list is not a sentence. Notice how easily a colon
> corrects the problem. (See p. 58.)

If the fragmented phrase cannot be attached to a
nearby sentence, turn the phrase into a sentence. You may
need to add a subject, a verb, or both.

▶ If Eric doesn't get his way, he goes into a fit of rage.
For example, ~~lying~~ on the floor screaming or ~~opening~~
the cabinet doors and then ~~slamming~~ them shut.

> The writer corrected this fragment by adding a subject —
> *he* — and substituting verbs for the verbals *lying*, *opening*,
> and *slamming*.

14c. Acceptable fragments

Skilled writers occasionally use sentence fragments for
emphasis. In the following passage, Richard Rodriguez
uses a fragment (italicized) to draw attention to his
mother.

> Following the dramatic Americanization of their chil-
> dren, even my parents grew more publicly confident.
> *Especially my mother.* She learned the names of all the
> people on our block.   — *Hunger of Memory*

Although fragments are sometimes appropriate,
writers and readers do not always agree on when they are
appropriate. Therefore, you will find it safer to write in
complete sentences.

15. Revise comma splices and fused sentences.

When a writer puts no mark of punctuation and no coordinating conjunction (*and*, *but*, *or*, *nor*, *for*, *so*, *yet*) between independent clauses, the result is a fused sentence (also called a *run-on sentence*). An independent clause is a word group that can stand alone as a sentence.

	INDEPENDENT CLAUSE	INDEPENDENT CLAUSE
FUSED	Power tends to corrupt	absolute power corrupts absolutely.

A far more common error is the comma splice — independent clauses separated by a comma without a coordinating conjunction.

COMMA SPLICE	Power tends to corrupt, absolute power corrupts absolutely.
COMMA SPLICE	Power tends to corrupt, moreover, absolute power corrupts absolutely.

In the second example, *moreover* is a conjunctive adverb, not a coordinating conjunction. (See p. 40.)

If two independent clauses are to appear in one sentence, they must be joined by a comma and a coordinating conjunction (*and*, *but*, *or*, *nor*, *for*, *so*, *yet*) or by a semicolon (or occasionally a colon).

REVISED	Power tends to corrupt, and absolute power corrupts absolutely.
REVISED	Power tends to corrupt; absolute power corrupts absolutely.

To correct a comma splice or a fused sentence, you have four choices:

1. Use a comma and a coordinating conjunction.
2. Use a semicolon (or, if appropriate, a colon).
3. Make the clauses into separate sentences.
4. Restructure the sentence, perhaps by subordinating one of the clauses.

One of these revision techniques will usually work better than the others for a particular sentence. The fourth technique, the one requiring the most extensive revision, is frequently the most effective.

15a. Revision with a comma and a coordinating conjunction

There are seven coordinating conjunctions in English: *and*, *but*, *or*, *nor*, *for*, *so*, and *yet*. When a coordinating conjunction joins independent clauses, it is usually preceded by a comma.

▶ Most of his contemporaries had made plans for their
retirement, *but* Tom had not.

15b. Revision with a semicolon

When the independent clauses are closely related and their relation is clear without a coordinating conjunction, a semicolon is an acceptable method of revision.

▶ The suburbs seemed cold*;* they lacked the warmth

and excitement of our Italian neighborhood.

A semicolon is required between independent clauses that have been linked with a conjunctive adverb such as *however* or *therefore* or a transitional phrase such as *in fact* or *of course*. (See p. 57 for a more complete list.)

▶ The timber wolf looks like a large German shepherd*;*

however, the wolf has longer legs, larger feet, and a

wider head.

15c. Revision by separating sentences

If both independent clauses are long — or if one is a question and the other is not — consider making them separate sentences.

▶ Why should we pay taxes to support public trans-
portation*? We* we prefer to save energy by carpooling.

15d. Revision by restructuring the sentence

For sentence variety, consider restructuring the sentence, perhaps by turning one of the independent clauses into a subordinate clause or phrase.

▶ Wind power is a supplemental source of energy/ ~~it~~ can
   that
   be combined with electricity, gas, or solar energy.

▶ It was obvious that Paula had been out walking in the
   woods her boots were covered with mud and leaves.
   because

16. If English is not your native language, check for common ESL problems.

This section of *A Pocket Style Manual* has a special audience: speakers of English as a second language (ESL) who have learned English but continue to have difficulty with a few troublesome features of the language.

16a. Articles

The definite article *the* and the indefinite articles *a* and *an* signal that a noun is about to appear. The noun may follow the article immediately or modifiers may intervene.

> *the cat, the* black *cat*
> *a sunset, a* spectacular *sunset*
> *an apple, an* appetizing *apple*

When to use a (*or* an).   Use *a* or *an* with singular count nouns whose specific identity is not known to the reader. Count nouns refer to persons, places, or things that can be counted: *one girl, two girls; one city, three cities.*

▶ Mary Beth arrived in limousine.
   a

▶ We are looking for apartment close to the lake.
   an

A (or *an*) usually means "one among many" but can also mean "any one."

NOTE: *A* is used before a consonant sound: *a banana*, *a happy child*. *An* is used before a vowel sound: *an eggplant*, *an honorable person*. See the Glossary of Usage.

When not to use a (or an).   *A* (or *an*) is not used to mark noncount nouns. Noncount nouns refer to entities or abstractions that cannot be counted: *water*, *silver*, *sugar*, *furniture*, *patience*. (See below for a fuller list.)

▶ Claudia asked her mother for ~~an~~ advice.

If you want to express an amount of something designated by a noncount noun, you can often add a quantifier in front of it: *a quart of milk*, *an ounce of gold*, *a piece of furniture*.

NOTE: A few noncount nouns may also be used as count nouns: *Bill loves lemonade; Bill offered me a lemonade.*

> **COMMONLY USED NONCOUNT NOUNS**
>
> *Food and drink*: bacon, beef, bread, broccoli, butter, cabbage, candy, cauliflower, celery, cereal, cheese, chicken, chocolate, coffee, corn, cream, fish, flour, fruit, ice cream, lemonade, lettuce, meat, milk, oil, pasta, rice, salt, spinach, sugar, tea, water, wine, yogurt
>
> *Nonfood substances*: air, cement, coal, dirt, gasoline, gold, paper, petroleum, plastic, rain, silver, snow, soap, steel, wood, wool
>
> *Abstract nouns:* advice, anger, beauty, confidence, courage, employment, fun, happiness, health, honesty, information, intelligence, knowledge, love, poverty, satisfaction, truth, wealth
>
> *Other*: biology (and other areas of study), clothing, equipment, furniture, homework, jewelry, luggage, lumber, machinery, mail, money, news, poetry, pollution, research, scenery, traffic, transportation, violence, weather, work

When to use the.   Use the definite article *the* with most nouns whose specific identity is known to the reader. Usually the identity will be clear for one of these reasons:

1. The noun has been previously mentioned.
2. A word group following the noun restricts its identity.
3. The context or situation makes the noun's identity clear.

▶ A truck loaded with dynamite cut in front of our van.
the
When truck skidded a few seconds later, we almost
∧
plowed into it.

The noun *truck* is preceded by *A* when it is first mentioned. When the noun is mentioned again, it is preceded by *the* since readers now know the specific truck being discussed.

▶ Bob warned me that *the* gun on the top shelf of the cup-
∧
board was loaded.

The phrase *on the top shelf of the cupboard* identifies the specific gun.

▶ Please don't slam *the* door when you leave.
∧

Both the speaker and the listener know which door is meant.

When not to use the.   Do not use *the* with plural or noncount nouns meaning "all" or "in general."

▶ ~~The~~ *F* fountains are an expensive element of landscape

design.

▶ In some parts of the world, ~~the~~ rice is preferred to all

other grains.

Although there are many exceptions, do not use *the* with most singular proper nouns: names of persons (Jessica Webner); names of streets, squares, parks, cities, and states (Prospect Street, Union Square, Denali National Park, Miami, Idaho); names of continents and most countries (South America, Italy); and names of bays and single lakes, mountains, and islands (Tampa Bay, Lake Geneva, Mount Everest, Crete).

Exceptions to this rule include names of large regions, deserts, and peninsulas (the East Coast, the Sahara, the Iberian Peninsula) and names of oceans, seas, gulfs, canals, and rivers (the Pacific, the Dead Sea, the Persian Gulf, the Panama Canal, the Amazon).

NOTE: *The* is used to mark plural proper nouns: the United Nations, the Finger Lakes, the Andes, the Bahamas.

16b. Helping verbs and main verbs

Only certain combinations of helping verbs and main verbs make sense in English. The correct combinations are discussed in this section, after the following review of helping verbs and main verbs.

Review. Helping verbs always appear before main verbs.

HV MV   HV   MV
We *will leave* for the picnic at noon. *Do* you *want* a ride?

There are twenty-three helping verbs in English. Nine of them, called *modals*, function only as helping verbs. The others — forms of *do*, *have*, and *be* — function either as helping or as main verbs.

HELPING VERBS

Modals: can, could, may, might, must, shall, should, will, would

Forms of do: do, does, did

Forms of have: have, has, had

Forms of be: be, am, is, are, was, were, being, been

Every main verb has five forms (except *be*, which has eight). The following list shows these forms for the regular verb *help* and the irregular verb *give*. (See pp. 22–24 for a list of common irregular verbs.)

BASE FORM	help, give
***-S* FORM**	helps, gives
PAST TENSE	helped, gave
PAST PARTICIPLE	helped, given
PRESENT PARTICIPLE	helping, giving

Modal + base form. After the modals *can*, *could*, *may*, *might*, *must*, *shall*, *should*, *will*, and *would*, use the base form of the verb.

▶ My cousin will send̸s us photographs from her

wedding.

> We could ~~spoke~~ ^{speak} Spanish when we were young.

Do, does, *or* **did + *base form.*** After helping verbs that are a form of *do*, use the base form of the verb.

> Mariko does not wants/ any more dessert.

> Did Janice ~~bought~~ ^{buy} the gift for Katherine?

Have, has, *or* **had + *past participle.*** To form one of the perfect tenses, use *have*, *has*, or *had* followed by a past participle (usually ending in *-ed*, *-d*, *-en*, *-n*, or *-t*). (See perfect tenses, p. 25.)

> Many churches have ~~offer~~ ^{offered} shelter to the homeless.

> An-Mei has not ~~speaking~~ ^{spoken} Chinese since she was a child.

Form of* be + *present participle. To express an action in progress, use *am*, *is*, *are*, *was*, *were*, *be*, or *been* followed by a present participle (the *-ing* form of the verb).

> Carlos is ~~build~~ ^{building} his house on a cliff overlooking the ocean.

> Uncle Roy was ~~driven~~ ^{driving} a brand new red Corvette.

The helping verbs *be* and *been* must be preceded by other helping verbs. See the progressive forms listed on page 25.

CAUTION: Certain verbs are not normally used in the progressive sense in English. In general, these verbs express a state of being or mental activity, not a dynamic action. Common examples are *appear*, *believe*, *have*, *hear*, *know*, *like*, *need*, *see*, *seem*, *taste*, *think*, *understand*, and *want*.

> I ~~am wanting~~ ^{want} to see August Wilson's *Fences* at Arena Stage.

Form of* be + *past participle. To form the passive voice, use *am, are, was, were, being, be,* or *been* followed by a past participle (usually ending in *-ed, -d, -en, -n,* or *-t*). When a sentence is written in the passive voice, the subject of the sentence receives the action instead of doing it. (See p. 26.)

► *Bleak House* was ~~write~~ *written* by Charles Dickens.

► The scientists were ~~honor~~ *honored* for their work with endangered species.

In the passive voice, the helping verb *be* must be preceded by a modal: Senator Dixon *will be defeated. Being* must be preceded by *am, is, are, was,* or *were*: The child *was being teased. Been* must be preceded by *have, has,* or *had*: I *have been invited* to a party.

CAUTION: Although they may seem to have passive meanings, verbs such as *occur, happen, sleep, die,* and *fall* may not be used to form the passive voice because they are intransitive. Only transitive verbs, those that take direct objects, may be used to form the passive voice.

► The earthquake ~~was~~ occurred last Friday.

16c. Omitted subjects, expletives, or verbs

Some languages allow omission of subjects, expletives, or verbs in certain contexts. English does not.

English requires a subject for all sentences except imperatives, in which the subject *you* is understood (*Give to the poor*). If your native language allows the omission of an explicit subject, be especially alert to this requirement in English.

► ~~Have~~ *I have* a large collection of baseball cards.

► My brother is very bright; *he* could read a book before he started school.

When the subject has been moved from its normal position before the verb, English sometimes requires an expletive (*there* or *it*) at the beginning of the sentence or clause.

▶ As you know, ~~are~~ many religious sects in India.
there

▶ ~~Is~~ healthy to eat fruit and grains.
It is

The subjects of these sentences are *sects* and *to eat fruit and grains*.

Although some languages allow the omission of the verb when the meaning is clear without it, English does not.

▶ Powell Street in San Francisco very steep.
is

16d. Repeated subjects or objects

English does not allow a subject to be repeated in its own clause. This is true even if a word group intervenes between the subject and the verb.

▶ The painting that had been stolen ~~it~~ was found.

The pronoun *it* repeats the subject *painting*.

In some languages an object is repeated later in the adjective clause in which it appears; in English, such repetitions are not allowed. Adjective clauses usually begin with *who*, *whom*, *whose*, *which*, or *that*, and these words always serve a grammatical function within the clauses they introduce. Another word in the clause cannot also serve that same function.

▶ The puppy ran after the taxi that we were riding in ~~it~~.

The relative pronoun *that* is the object of the preposition *in*, so the object *it* is not allowed.

Even when the relative pronoun has been omitted, do not add another word with its same function.

▶ The puppy ran after the taxi we were riding in ~~it~~.

The relative pronoun *that* is understood.

Punctuation

17. The comma

The comma was invented to help readers. Without it, sentence parts can collide into one another unexpectedly, causing misreadings.

CONFUSING   If you cook Elmer will do the dishes.

CONFUSING   While we were eating a rattlesnake
approached our campsite.

Add commas in the logical places (after *cook* and *eating*), and suddenly all is clear. No longer is Elmer being cooked, the rattlesnake being eaten.

Various rules have evolved to prevent such misreadings and to guide readers through complex grammatical structures. According to most experts, you should use a comma in the following situations.

17a. Before a coordinating conjunction joining independent clauses

When a coordinating conjunction connects two or more independent clauses — word groups that could stand alone as separate sentences — a comma must precede it. There are seven coordinating conjunctions in English: *and*, *but*, *or*, *nor*, *for*, *so*, and *yet*.

A comma tells readers that one independent clause has come to a close and that another is about to begin.

▶ Nearly everyone has heard of love at first sight, but I

fell in love at first dance.

EXCEPTION: If the two independent clauses are short and there is no danger of misreading, the comma may be omitted.

The plane took off and we were on our way.

CAUTION: Do *not* use a comma to separate compound elements that are not independent clauses. See page 55.

17b. After an introductory word group

Use a comma after an introductory adverb clause, adverb phrase, or participial phrase. A comma tells readers that the introductory word group has come to a close and that the main part of the sentence is about to begin.

▶ When Irwin was ready to eat‚ his cat jumped onto the

table.

▶ Near a small stream at the bottom of the canyon‚ we

discovered an abandoned shelter.

▶ Excited about the move‚ Alice and Don began packing

their books.

EXCEPTION: The comma may be omitted after a short clause or phrase if there is no danger of misreading.

In no time we were at 2,800 feet.

17c. Between items in a series

Use a comma between all items in a series, including the last two.

▶ For breakfast the children ordered cornflakes, English

muffins with peanut butter‚ and cherry Cokes.

Although some writers view the comma between the last two items as optional, most experts advise using it because its omission can result in ambiguity or misreading.

17d. Between coordinate adjectives

Use a comma between coordinate adjectives, those that each modify a noun separately.

▶ Robert is a warm‚ gentle‚ affectionate father.

Adjectives are coordinate if they can be connected with *and*: *warm and gentle and affectionate.*

CAUTION: Do not use a comma between cumulative adjectives, those that do not each modify the noun separately.

Three large gray shapes moved slowly toward us.

Adjectives are cumulative if they cannot be connected with *and*. It would be very odd to say *three and large and gray shapes*.

17e. To set off a nonrestrictive element

A *restrictive* element restricts the meaning of the word it modifies and is therefore essential to the meaning of the sentence. It is not set off with commas. A *nonrestrictive* element describes a word whose meaning already is clear. It is not essential to the meaning of the sentence and is set off with commas.

RESTRICTIVE
For camp the children needed clothes *that were washable*.

NONRESTRICTIVE
For camp the children needed sturdy shoes, *which were expensive*.

If you remove a restrictive element from a sentence, the meaning changes significantly, becoming more general than intended. The writer of the first sample sentence does not mean that the children needed clothes in general. The meaning is more restricted: the children needed *washable* clothes.

If you remove a nonrestrictive element from a sentence, the meaning does not change significantly. Some meaning is lost, to be sure, but the defining characteristics of the person or thing described remain the same as before. The children needed *sturdy shoes*, and these happened to be expensive.

Elements that may be restrictive or nonrestrictive include adjective clauses, adjective phrases, and appositives.

Adjective clauses. Adjective clauses, which usually follow the noun or pronoun they describe, begin with a relative pronoun (*who*, *whom*, *whose*, *which*, *that*) or a relative adverb (*when*, *where*). When an adjective clause is nonrestrictive, set it off with commas; when it is restrictive, omit the commas.

NONRESTRICTIVE CLAUSE

▶ Ed's country kitchen, which is located on thirteen acres, was completely furnished with bats in the rafters and mice in the kitchen.

RESTRICTIVE CLAUSE

▶ A corporation that has government contracts must maintain careful personnel records.

NOTE: Use *that* only with restrictive clauses. Many writers use *which* only with nonrestrictive clauses, but usage varies.

Adjective phrases. Prepositional or verbal phrases functioning as adjectives may be restrictive or nonrestrictive. Nonrestrictive phrases are set off with commas; restrictive phrases are not.

NONRESTRICTIVE PHRASE

▶ The helicopter, with its 100,000-candlepower spotlight illuminating the area, circled above.

RESTRICTIVE PHRASE

▶ One corner of the attic was filled with newspapers dating from the turn of the century.

Appositives. An appositive is a noun or pronoun that renames a nearby noun. Nonrestrictive appositives are set off with commas; restrictive appositives are not.

NONRESTRICTIVE APPOSITIVE

▶ Norman Mailer's first novel, *The Naked and the Dead*, was a best-seller.

RESTRICTIVE APPOSITIVE

▶ The song "Fire It Up" was blasted out of amplifiers ten feet tall.

17f. To set off transitional and parenthetical expressions, absolute phrases, and contrasted elements

Transitional expressions. Transitional expressions serve as bridges between sentences or parts of sentences. They include conjunctive adverbs such as *however*, *therefore*, and *moreover* and transitional phrases such as *for example* and *as a matter of fact*. For a more complete list, see page 57.

When a transitional expression appears between independent clauses in a compound sentence, it is preceded by a semicolon and usually followed by a comma.

▶ Minh did not understand our language; moreover, he

was unfamiliar with our customs.

When a transitional expression appears at the beginning of a sentence or in the middle of an independent clause, it is usually set off with commas.

▶ As a matter of fact, American football was established

by fans who wanted to play a more organized game of

football.

▶ The prospective babysitter looked very promising; she

was busy, however, throughout January.

Parenthetical expressions. Expressions that are distinctly parenthetical, interrupting the flow of a sentence, should be set off with commas.

▶ Evolution, so far as we know, does not work this way.

Absolute phrases. An absolute phrase, which modifies the whole sentence, should be set off with commas.

▶ His tennis game at last perfected, Chris won the cup.

Contrasted elements. Sharp contrasts beginning with words such as *not* and *unlike* are set off with commas.

▶ Celia, unlike Robert, had no loathing for dance
  contests.

17g. To set off nouns of direct address, the words *yes* and *no*, interrogative tags, and mild interjections

▶ Forgive us, Dr. Spock, for spanking Brian.

▶ Yes, the loan will probably be approved.

▶ The film was faithful to the book, wasn't it?

▶ Well, cases like this are difficult to decide.

17h. To set off direct quotations introduced with expressions such as *he said*

▶ Naturalist Arthur Cleveland Bent remarked, "In part
  the peregrine declined unnoticed because it is not
  adorable."

17i. With dates, addresses, titles

Dates.   In dates, the year is set off from the rest of the sentence with commas.

▶ On December 12, 1890, orders were sent out for the
  arrest of Sitting Bull.

EXCEPTIONS: Commas are not needed if the date is inverted or if only the month and year are given: The deadline is 15 April 1994. May 1992 was a surprisingly cold month.

Addresses.   The elements of an address or place name are followed by commas. A zip code, however, is not preceded by a comma.

▶ Greg lived at 708 Spring Street, Washington, Illinois
  61571.

Titles.   If a title follows a name, separate it from the rest of the sentence with a pair of commas.

▶ Sandra Barnes , M.D. , performed the surgery.
　　　　　　　　∧　　　　∧

17j. Misuses of the comma

Do not use commas unless you have a good reason for using them. In particular, avoid using the comma in the following situations.

BETWEEN COMPOUND ELEMENTS THAT ARE NOT INDEPENDENT CLAUSES

▶ The director led the cast members to their positions/

and gave an inspiring last-minute pep talk.

TO SEPARATE A VERB FROM ITS SUBJECT

▶ Zoos large enough to give the animals freedom to

roam/ are becoming more popular.

BETWEEN CUMULATIVE ADJECTIVES (See p. 50.)

▶ Joyce was wearing a slinky/ red silk gown.

TO SET OFF RESTRICTIVE ELEMENTS (See pp. 51–52.)

▶ Drivers/ who think they own the road/ make cycling

a dangerous sport.

AFTER A COORDINATING CONJUNCTION

▶ Occasionally soap operas are live, but/ more often

they are taped.

AFTER *SUCH AS* OR *LIKE*

▶ Plants such as/ begonias and impatiens add color to a

shady garden.

BEFORE *THAN*

▶ Touring Crete was more thrilling for us/ than visiting

the Greek islands frequented by the jet set.

BEFORE A PARENTHESIS

▶ At MCI Sylvia began at the bottom/ (with only a

 cubicle and a swivel chair), but within five years she

 had been promoted to supervisor.

TO SET OFF AN INDIRECT (REPORTED) QUOTATION

▶ Samuel Goldwyn once said/ that a verbal contract isn't

 worth the paper it's written on.

WITH A QUESTION MARK OR AN EXCLAMATION POINT

▶ "Why don't you try it?/" she coaxed.

18. The semicolon and the colon

18a. The semicolon

The semicolon is used between independent clauses not
joined by a coordinating conjunction. It can also be used
between items in a series containing internal punctuation.

   The semicolon is never used between elements of un-
equal grammatical rank.

Between independent clauses. When related independent clauses appear in one sentence, they are ordinarily connected with a comma and a coordinating conjunction
(*and*, *but*, *or*, *nor*, *for*, *so*, *yet*). The coordinating conjunction expresses the relation between the clauses. If the relation is clear without a conjunction, a writer may choose
to connect the clauses with a semicolon instead.

> Injustice is relatively easy to bear; what stings is
> justice.   —H. L. Mencken

   A writer may also choose to connect the clauses with
a semicolon and a conjunctive adverb such as *however* or
therefore or a transitional phrase such as *for example* or
in fact.

> He swallowed a lot of wisdom; however, it seemed as if
> all of it had gone down the wrong way.
>   —G. C. Lichtenberg

CONJUNCTIVE ADVERBS

accordingly, also, anyway, besides, certainly, consequently, conversely, finally, furthermore, hence, however, incidentally, indeed, instead, likewise, meanwhile,
moreover, nevertheless, next, nonetheless, otherwise,
similarly, specifically, still, subsequently, then, therefore, thus

TRANSITIONAL PHRASES

after all, as a matter of fact, as a result, at any rate, at
the same time, even so, for example, for instance, in
addition, in conclusion, in fact, in other words, in the
first place, on the contrary, on the other hand

CAUTION: A semicolon must be used whenever a coordinating conjunction has been omitted between independent
clauses. To use merely a comma — or to use a comma and
a conjunctive adverb or transitional expression — creates
an error known as a comma splice. (See pp. 39–41.)

▶ Some visitors were new; others had been there before.

*Between items in a series containing internal punc-
tuation.*   Ordinarily, items in a series are separated by
commas. If one or more of the items contains internal
punctuation, however, a writer may use semicolons
instead.

> The only sensible ends of literature are first, the plea-
> surable toil of writing; second, the gratification of one's
> family and friends; and lastly, the solid cash.
>   — Nathaniel Hawthorne

Misuses of the semicolon.   Do not use a semicolon in
the following situations.

**BETWEEN A SUBORDINATE CLAUSE AND THE REST OF
THE SENTENCE**

▶ Unless you brush your teeth within ten or fifteen min-

   utes after eating, brushing does almost no good.

BETWEEN AN APPOSITIVE AND THE WORD IT REFERS TO

▶ Another delicious dish is the chef's special, a roasted

   duck rubbed with spices and stuffed with wild rice.

TO INTRODUCE A LIST

▶ Some of my favorite artists are featured on *Red, Hot,*

and Blue; the Neville Brothers, Annie Lennox, and

k. d. lang.

BETWEEN INDEPENDENT CLAUSES JOINED BY *AND, BUT,
OR, NOR, FOR, SO,* OR *YET*

▶ Five of the applicants had worked with spreadsheets;

but only one was familiar with database management.

18b. The colon

The colon is used after an independent clause to call attention to the words that follow it. The colon also has certain conventional uses.

To call attention to the words that follow it.   After an independent clause, a writer may use a colon to direct the reader's attention to a list, an appositive, or a quotation.

A LIST
The routine includes the following: twenty knee bends, fifty leg lifts, and five minutes of running in place.

AN APPOSITIVE
My roommate is guilty of two of the seven deadly sins: gluttony and sloth.

A QUOTATION
Consider the words of John F. Kennedy: "Ask not what your country can do for you; ask what you can do for your country."

For other ways of introducing quotations, see pages 63–64.

A colon may also be used between independent clauses if the second summarizes or explains the first.

Faith is like love: It cannot be forced.

Conventional uses.   Use a colon after the salutation in a formal letter, to indicate hours and minutes, to show proportions, between a title and subtitle, and to separate city and date in bibliographic entries.

Dear Sir or Madam:

5:30 P.M. (or p.m.)

The ratio of women to men was 2:1.

*The Glory of Hera: Greek Mythology and the Greek
Family*

Boston: Bedford, 1993

NOTE: In biblical references, a colon is ordinarily used
between chapter and verse (Luke 2:14). The Modern Language Association recommends a period (Luke 2.14).

Misuses of the colon.   A colon must be preceded by an
independent clause. Therefore, avoid using it in the following situations.

BETWEEN A VERB AND ITS OBJECT OR COMPLEMENT

▶ Some important vitamins found in vegetables are/

vitamin A, thiamine, niacin, and vitamin C.

BETWEEN A PREPOSITION AND ITS OBJECT

▶ The area to be painted consisted of/ three gable ends,

trim work, six windows, and a back porch.

AFTER *SUCH AS*, *INCLUDING*, OR *FOR EXAMPLE*

▶ The trees on campus include fine Japanese specimens

such as/ black pines, ginkgos, and cutleaf maples.

19. The apostrophe

The apostrophe is used to indicate possession and to mark
contractions. In addition, it has a few conventional uses.

19a. To indicate possession

The apostrophe is used to indicate that a noun is possessive. Possessive nouns usually indicate ownership, as in
Tim's hat or *the editor's desk*. Frequently, however, ownership is only loosely implied: *the tree's roots*, *a day's*

work. If you are not sure whether a noun is possessive, try turning it into an *of* phrase: *the roots of the tree, the work of a day.*

When to add -'s.   Add -'*s* if the noun does not end in -*s* or if the noun is singular and ends in -*s*.

> Thank you for refunding the children's money.

> Lois's sister spent last year in India.

EXCEPTION: If pronunciation would be awkward with the added -'*s*, some writers use only the apostrophe: Sophocles' plays are among my favorites. Either use is acceptable.

When to add only an apostrophe.   If the noun is plural and ends in -*s*, add only an apostrophe.

> Both diplomats' briefcases were stolen.

Joint possession.   To show joint possession, use -'*s* (or -*s*') with the last noun only; to show individual possession, make all nouns possessive.

> Have you seen Joyce and Greg's new camper?

> John's and Marie's expectations were quite different.

Compound nouns.   If a noun is compound, use -'*s* (or -*s*') with the last element.

> Her father-in-law's sculpture won first place.

Indefinite pronouns such as someone.   Use -'*s* to indicate that an indefinite pronoun is possessive. Indefinite pronouns refer to no specific person or thing: *everyone, someone, no one,* and so on.

> Someone's raincoat has been left behind.

19b. To mark contractions

In a contraction, an apostrophe takes the place of missing letters.

> It's a shame that Frank can't go on the tour.

It's stands for *it is, can't* for *cannot.*

The apostrophe is also used to mark the omission of the first two digits of a year (*the class of '96*) or years (*the '60s generation*).

19c. Conventional uses

An apostrophe may be used to pluralize numbers mentioned as numbers, letters mentioned as letters, words mentioned as words, and abbreviations.

> Peggy skated nearly perfect figure 8's.

> Two large red *J*'s were painted on the door.

> We've heard enough *maybe*'s.

> You must ask to see their I.D.'s.

EXCEPTION: An *-s* alone is often added to the years in a decade: the 1990s.

19d. Misuses of the apostrophe

Do not use an apostrophe in the following situations.

WITH NOUNS THAT ARE NOT POSSESSIVE

> ▶ Some ~~outpatient's~~ are given special parking permits.
>   *outpatients*

IN THE POSSESSIVE PRONOUNS *ITS, WHOSE, HIS, HERS, OURS, YOURS,* AND *THEIRS*

> ▶ Each area has ~~it's~~ own conference room.
>   *its*

> *It's* means *it is.* The possessive pronoun *its* contains no apostrophe despite the fact that it is possessive.

20. Quotation marks

Quotation marks are used to enclose direct quotations. They are also used around some titles and to set off words used as words.

20a. To enclose direct quotations

Direct quotations of a person's words, whether spoken or written, must be in quotation marks.

> "A foolish consistency is the hobgoblin of little minds," wrote Ralph Waldo Emerson.

EXCEPTION: When a long quotation has been set off from the text by indenting, quotation marks are not needed. See page 88.

Use single quotation marks to enclose a quotation within a quotation.

> According to Paul Eliott, Eskimo hunters "chant an ancient magic song to the seal they are after: 'Beast of the sea! Come and place yourself before me in the early morning!' "

20b. Around titles of short works

Use quotation marks around titles of newspaper and magazine articles, poems, short stories, songs, episodes of television and radio programs, and chapters or subdivisions of books.

> The poem "Mother to Son" is by Langston Hughes.

NOTE: Titles of books, plays, and films and names of magazines and newspapers are put in italics or underlined. See page 75.

20c. To set off words used as words

Although words used as words are ordinarily underlined to indicate italics, quotation marks are also acceptable.

> The words "flaunt" and "flout" are frequently confused.

> The words *flaunt* and *flout* are frequently confused.

20d. Other punctuation with quotation marks

This section describes the conventions to observe in placing various marks of punctuation inside or outside quotation marks. It also explains how to punctuate when introducing quoted material.

Periods and commas. Always place periods and commas inside quotation marks.

> "This is a stick-up," said the well-dressed young couple. "We want all your money."

This rule applies to single and double quotation marks, and it applies to all uses of quotation marks.

NOTE: MLA parenthetical citations are an exception to this rule. Put the parenthetical citation after the quotation mark and before the period: According to Kane, "Pollution has become a serious problem in most of our national parks" (5). See page 89.

Colons and semicolons.   Put colons and semicolons outside quotation marks.

> Harold wrote, "I regret that I cannot attend the AIDS fundraiser"; his letter, however, contained a contribution.

Question marks and exclamation points.   Put question marks and exclamation points inside quotation marks unless they apply to the sentence as a whole.

> Contrary to tradition, bedtime at my house is marked by "Mommy, can I tell you a story now?"

> Have you heard the old proverb "Do not climb the hill until you reach it"?

In the first sentence, the question mark applies only to the quoted question. In the second sentence, the question mark applies to the whole sentence.

NOTE: MLA parenthetical citations create a special problem. According to MLA, the question mark or exclamation point should appear before the quotation mark, and a period should follow the parenthetical citation: Rosie Thomas asks, "Is nothing in life ever straight and clear, the way children see it?" (77).

Introducing quoted material.   After a word group introducing a quotation, use a colon, a comma, or no punctuation at all, whichever is appropriate in context.

If a quotation has been formally introduced, a colon is appropriate. A formal introduction is a full independent clause, not just an expression such as *he said* or *she remarked*.

> Morrow views personal ads as an art form: "The personal ad is like haiku of self-celebration, a brief solo played on one's own horn."

If a quotation is introduced or followed by an expression such as *he said* or *she remarked*, use a comma.

> Robert Frost said, "You can be a little ungrammatical if you come from the right part of the country."

"You can be a little ungrammatical if you come from the right part of the country," said Robert Frost.

When you blend a quotation into your own sentence, use either a comma or no punctuation, depending on the way in which the quotation fits into the sentence structure.

The future champion could, as he put it, "float like a butterfly and sting like a bee."

Hudson noted that the prisoners escaped "by squeezing through a tiny window eighteen feet above the floor of their cell."

If a quotation appears at the beginning of a sentence, set it off with a comma unless the quotation ends with a question mark or an exclamation point.

"We shot them like dogs," boasted Davy Crockett, who was among Jackson's troops.

"What is it?" I asked, bracing myself.

If a quoted sentence is interrupted by explanatory words, use commas to set off the explanatory words.

"A great many people think they are thinking," wrote William James, "when they are merely rearranging their prejudices."

If two successive quoted sentences from the same source are interrupted by explanatory words, use a comma before the explanatory words and a period after them.

"I was a flop as a daily reporter," admitted E. B. White. "Every piece had to be a masterpiece—and before you knew it, Tuesday was Wednesday."

20e. Misuses of quotation marks

Do not use quotation marks to draw attention to familiar slang, to disown trite expressions, or to justify an attempt at humor.

▶ Between Thanksgiving and Super Bowl Sunday, many

American wives become "football widows."

Do not use quotation marks around indirect quotations. Indirect quotations report a person's words instead of quoting them directly.

▶ After leaving the scene of the domestic quarrel, the officer said that /"he was due for a coffee break."\

Do not use quotation marks around the title of your own essay.

21. Other marks

21a. The period

Use a period to end all sentences except direct questions or genuine exclamations. Use a period, not a question mark, for an indirect question — that is, a reported question.

Celia asked whether the picnic would be canceled.

A period is conventionally used in abbreviations such as the following.

Mr.	B.A.	B.C.	i.e.	A.M. (or a.m.)
Ms.	Ph.D.	B.C.E.	e.g.	P.M. (or p.m.)
Dr.	R.N.	A.D.	etc.	

A period is not used with U.S. Postal Service abbreviations for states: MD, TX, CA.

Ordinarily a period is not used in abbreviations of organization names.

NATO	IRS	AFL-CIO	FCC
USA (or	NAACP	PUSH	IBM
U.S.A.)	UCLA	NBA	NIH

Usage varies, however. When in doubt, consult a dictionary, a style manual, or a publication by the agency in question. Even the yellow pages can help.

NOTE: If a sentence ends with a period marking an abbreviation, do not add a second period.

21b. The question mark

Use a question mark after a direct question.

What is the horsepower of a 747 engine?

If a polite request is written in the form of a question, you may use a question mark, though usage varies.

> Would you please send me your catalog of lilies?

CAUTION: Use a period, not a question mark, after an indirect question, one that is reported rather than asked directly.

> He asked me where the nearest pastry shop was.

21c. The exclamation point

Use an exclamation point after a sentence that expresses exceptional feeling or deserves special emphasis.

> The medic shook me and kept yelling, "He's dead! He's dead! Can't you see that?"

CAUTION: Do not overuse the exclamation point.

> ▶ In the fisherman's memory the fish lives on, increasing
>
> in length and weight with each passing year, until at
>
> last it is big enough to shade a fishing boat⟋.

This sentence doesn't need to be pumped up with an exclamation point. It is emphatic enough without it.

21d. The dash

The dash may be used to set off material that deserves special emphasis. When typing, use two hyphens to form a dash (--), with no spaces before or after them.

Use a dash to introduce a list, a restatement, an amplification, or a dramatic shift in tone or thought.

> Along the wall are the bulk liquids — sesame seed oil, honey, safflower oil, and half-liquid peanut butter.

> Consider the amount of sugar in the average person's diet — 104 pounds per year.

> Kiere took a few steps back, came running full speed, kicked a mighty kick — and missed the ball.

In the first two examples, the writer could also use a colon. (See p. 58.) The colon is more formal than the dash and not quite as dramatic.

Use a pair of dashes to set off parenthetical material that deserves special emphasis or to set off an appositive that contains commas.

Everything that went wrong—from the peeping Tom at her window to my head-on collision—was blamed on our move.

In my hometown the basic needs of people—food, clothing, and shelter—are less costly than in Denver.

CAUTION: Unless you have a specific reason for using the dash, avoid it. Unnecessary dashes create a choppy effect.

▶ Seeing that our young people learn to use computers makes good sense. Herding them ⁄ sheeplike ⁄ into computer technology does not.

21e. Parentheses

Use parentheses to enclose supplemental material, minor digressions, and afterthoughts.

After taking her temperature, pulse, and blood pressure (routine vital signs), the nurse made Becky comfortable.

Use parentheses to enclose letters or numbers labeling items in a series.

There are three points of etiquette in poker: (1) always allow someone to cut the cards, (2) don't forget to ante up, and (3) never stack your chips.

CAUTION: Do not overuse parentheses. Often a sentence reads more gracefully without them.

▶ Researchers have said that ~~ten million (estimates run~~ *from ten to fifty million* ∧ ~~as high as fifty million)~~ Americans have hypoglycemia.

21f. Brackets

Use brackets to enclose any words or phrases inserted into an otherwise word-for-word quotation.

Audubon reports that "if there are not enough young to balance deaths, the end of the species [California condor] is inevitable."

The *Audubon* article did not contain the words *California condor* in the sentence quoted.

The Latin word *sic* in brackets indicates that an error in a quoted sentence appears in the original source.

According to the review, Kistler's performance was brilliant, "exceding [*sic*] the expectations of even her most loyal fans."

21g. The ellipsis mark

Use an ellipsis mark, three spaced periods, to indicate that you have deleted material from an otherwise word-for-word quotation.

> Reuben reports that "when the amount of cholesterol circulating in the blood rises over . . . 300 milligrams per 100, the chances of a heart attack increase dramatically."

If you delete a full sentence or more in the middle of a quoted passage, use a period before the three ellipsis dots.

CAUTION: Do not use the ellipsis mark at the beginning of a quotation; do not use it at the end of a quotation unless you have cut some words from the end of the final sentence quoted.

21h. The slash

Use the slash to separate two or three lines of poetry that have been run in with your text. Add a space both before and after the slash.

> In the opening lines of "Jordan," George Herbert pokes gentle fun at popular poems of his time: "Who says that fictions only and false hair / Become a verse? Is there in truth no beauty?"

Use the slash sparingly, if at all, to separate options: *pass/fail*, *producer/director*. Put no space around the slash. Avoid using a slash for *he/she*, *and/or*, and *his/her*.

22. Capitalization

In addition to the following guidelines, a good dictionary can often tell you when to use capital letters.

22a. Proper versus common nouns

Proper nouns and words derived from them are capitalized; common nouns are not. Proper nouns name specific persons, places, and things. All other nouns are common nouns.

The following types of words are usually capitalized: names for the deity, religions, religious followers, sacred books; words of family relationships used as names; particular places; nationalities and their languages, races, tribes; educational institutions, departments, degrees, particular courses; government departments, organizations, political parties; and historical movements, periods, events, documents.

PROPER NOUNS	COMMON NOUNS
God (used as a name)	a god
Book of Jeremiah	a book
Grandmother Bishop	my grandmother
Father (used as a name)	my father
Lake Superior	a picturesque lake
the Capital Center	a center for advanced studies
the South	a southern state
Japan, a Japanese garden	an ornamental garden
University of Wisconsin	a good university
Veterans Administration	a federal agency
Phi Kappa Psi	a fraternity
a Democrat	an independent
the Enlightenment	the eighteenth century
the Declaration of Independence	a treaty

Months, holidays, and days of the week are capitalized: *May*, *Labor Day*, *Monday*. The seasons and numbers of the days of the month are not: *summer, the fifth of June*.

Names of school subjects are capitalized only if they are names of languages: *geology*, *English*. Names of particular courses are capitalized: *Geology 101*.

CAUTION: Do not capitalize common nouns to make them seem important: Our company is currently hiring computer programmers [*not* Company, Computer Programmers].

22b. Titles with proper names

Capitalize titles of persons when used as part of a proper name but usually not when used alone.

> Prof. Margaret Burnes; Dr. Harold Stevens; John Scott Williams, Jr.; Anne Tilton, LL.D.

> District Attorney Mill was ruled out of order.

> The district attorney was elected for a two-year term.

Usage varies when the title of an important public figure is used alone: The president [*or* President] vetoed the bill.

22c. Titles of works

In both titles and subtitles of works such as books, articles, and songs, major words should be capitalized. Minor words — articles, prepositions, and coordinating conjunctions — are not capitalized unless they are the first or last word of a title or subtitle. Capitalize the second part of a hyphenated term in a title only if it is a major word.

> *The Country of the Pointed Firs*

> "A Valediction: Of Weeping"

> *The F-Plan Diet*

22d. First word of a sentence or quoted sentence

The first word of a sentence should of course be capitalized. When quoting a sentence, capitalize the first word unless it is blended into the sentence that introduces it.

> In *Time* magazine Robert Hughes writes, "There are only about sixty Watteau paintings on whose authenticity all experts agree."

> Russell Baker has written that in our country "it is sport that is the opiate of the masses."

If a quoted sentence is interrupted by explanatory words, do not capitalize the first word after the interruption.

"If you wanted to go out," he said sharply, "you should have told me."

22e. First word following a colon

Do not capitalize the first word after a colon unless it begins an independent clause, in which case capitalization is optional.

> Most of the bar's patrons can be divided into two groups: the occasional after-work socializers and the regulars.

> This we are forced to conclude: The [*or* the] federal government is needed to protect the rights of minorities.

22f. Abbreviations

Capitalize abbreviations for departments and agencies of government, other organizations, and corporations; capitalize trade names and the call letters of radio and television stations.

> EPA, FBI, OPEC, IBM, Xerox, WCRB, KNBC-TV

23. Abbreviations, numbers, and italics (underlining)

23a. Abbreviations

Use abbreviations only when they are clearly appropriate.

Appropriate abbreviations.   Feel free to use standard abbreviations for titles immediately before and after proper names.

TITLES BEFORE PROPER NAMES	TITLES AFTER PROPER NAMES
Mr. Ralph Meyer	Thomas Hines, Jr.
Ms. Nancy Linehan	Anita Lor, Ph.D.
Dr. Margaret Simmons	Robert Simkowski, M.D.
Rev. John Stone	William Lyons, M.A.
St. Joan of Arc	Margaret Chin, LL.D.
Prof. James Russo	Polly Stern, D.D.S.

Do not abbreviate a title if it is not used with a proper name: My history professor [*not* prof.] was an expert on naval warfare.

Familiar abbreviations for the names of organizations, corporations, and countries are also acceptable.

> CIA, FBI, AFL-CIO, NAACP, IBM, UPI, CBS, USA (or U.S.A.)
>
> The YMCA has opened a new gym close to my office.

When using an unfamiliar abbreviation (such as CBE for Council of Biology Editors) throughout a paper, write the full name followed by the abbreviation in parentheses at the first mention of the name. You may use the abbreviation alone from then on.

Other commonly accepted abbreviations include B.C., A.D., A.M., P.M., No., and $. The abbreviation B.C. ("before Christ") follows a date, and A.D. (*anno Domini*) precedes a date. Acceptable alternatives are B.C.E. ("before the common era") and C.E. ("common era").

> 40 B.C. (or B.C.E.)   4:00 A.M. (or a.m.)   No. 12 (or no. 12)
> A.D. 44 (or C.E.)   6:00 P.M. (or p.m.) $150

Do not use these abbreviations, however, when they are not accompanied by a specific figure: We set off for the lake early in the morning [*not* A.M.].

Inappropriate abbreviations.   In formal writing, abbreviations for the following are not commonly accepted.

PERSONAL NAME   Charles [*not* Chas.]

UNITS OF MEASUREMENT   pound [*not* lb.]

DAYS OF THE WEEK   Monday [*not* Mon.]

HOLIDAYS   Christmas [*not* Xmas]

MONTHS   January, February, March [*not* Jan., Feb., Mar.]

COURSES OF STUDY   political science [*not* poli, sci.]

DIVISIONS OF WRITTEN WORKS   chapter, page [*not* ch., p.]

STATES AND COUNTRIES   Massachusetts [*not* MA or Mass.]

PARTS OF A BUSINESS NAME   Adams Lighting Company [*not* Adams Lighting Co.]; Kim and Brothers, Inc. [*not* Kim and Bros., Inc.]

Although Latin abbreviations are appropriate in foot-notes and bibliographies and in informal writing, use the appropriate English phrases in formal writing.

cf. (Latin *confer*, "compare")
e.g. (Latin *exempli gratia*, "for example")
et al. (Latin *et alii*, "and others")
etc. (Latin *et cetera*, "and so forth")
i.e. (Latin *id est*, "that is")
N.B. (Latin *nota bene*, "note well")

23b. Numbers

Spell out numbers of one or two words. Use figures for numbers that require more than two words to spell out.

▶ Now, some ~~8~~ *eight* years later, Muffin is still with us.

▶ I counted ~~one hundred seventy-six~~ *176* records on the shelf.

EXCEPTION: In technical and some business writing, fig-ures are preferred even when spellings would be brief, but usage varies.

If a sentence begins with a number, spell out the number or rewrite the sentence.

▶ ~~150~~ *One hundred fifty* children in our program need expensive dental treatment.

Generally, figures are acceptable for the following.

DATES   July 4, 1776, 56 B.C., A.D. 30

ADDRESSES   77 Latches Lane, 519 West 42nd Street

PERCENTAGES   55 percent (or 55%)

FRACTIONS, DECIMALS   ½, 0.047

SCORES   7 to 3, 21–18

STATISTICS   average age 37

SURVEYS   4 out of 5

EXACT AMOUNTS OF MONEY $105.37, $0.05

DIVISIONS OF BOOKS   volume 3, chapter 4, page 189

DIVISIONS OF PLAYS   Act I, scene i (or Act 1, scene 1)

IDENTIFICATION NUMBERS   serial no. 1098

TIME OF DAY   4:00 P.M., 1:30 A.M.

23c. Italics (underlining)

In handwritten or typed papers, <u>underlining</u> represents *italics*, a slanting typeface used in printed material.

Titles of works.   Titles of the following works are underlined to indicate italics.

TITLES OF BOOKS   *The Great Gatsby*, *A Distant Mirror*

MAGAZINES   *Time*, *Scientific American*

NEWSPAPERS   the *New York Times*, the *Boston Globe*

PAMPHLETS   *Common Sense*, *Facts about Marijuana*

LONG POEMS   *The Waste Land*, *Paradise Lost*

PLAYS   *King Lear*, *A Raisin in the Sun*

FILMS   *The Color Purple*, *Dances with Wolves*

TELEVISION PROGRAMS   *60 Minutes*

RADIO PROGRAMS   *All Things Considered*

MUSICAL COMPOSITIONS   Gershwin's *Porgy and Bess*

CHOREOGRAPHIC WORKS   Twyla Tharp's *Brief Fling*

WORKS OF VISUAL ART   Rodin's *The Thinker*

COMIC STRIPS   *Calvin and Hobbes*

SOFTWARE   *WordPerfect*

The titles of other works, such as short stories, essays, songs, and short poems, are enclosed in quotation marks. (See p. 62.)

NOTE: Do not underline the Bible or the titles of books in the Bible (Genesis, not *Genesis*); the titles of legal documents (the Constitution, not the *Constitution*); or the titles of your own papers.

Names of ships, trains, aircraft, spacecraft.   Underline names of specific ships, trains, aircraft, and spacecraft to indicate italics.

> *Challenger*, *Spirit of St. Louis*, *Queen Elizabeth II*, *Silver Streak*

▶ The success of the Soviet's <u>Sputnik</u> galvanized the U.S.

space program.

Foreign words.   Underline foreign words used in an
English sentence.

▶ Although Joe's method seemed to be successful, I de-

cided to establish my own <u>modus operandi.</u>

EXCEPTION: Do not underline foreign words that have become part of the English language — "laissez-faire," "fait
accompli," "habeas corpus," and "per diem," for example.

Words as words, etc.   Underline words used as words,
letters mentioned as letters, and numbers mentioned as
numbers.

▶ Tim assured us that the howling probably came from his

bloodhound, Billy, but his <u>probably</u> stuck in our minds.

▶ Sarah called her father by his given name, Johnny, but

she was unable to pronounce the <u>J.</u>

▶ A big <u>3</u> was painted on the door.

NOTE: Quotation marks may be used instead of underlining to set off words mentioned as words (See p. 62.)

Inappropriate underlining.   Underlining to emphasize
words or ideas is distracting and should be used sparingly.

▶ Tennis is a sport that has become an <u>addiction</u>.

24. Spelling and the hyphen

24a. Spelling

You learned to spell from repeated experience with words
in both reading and writing. Words have a look, a sound,
and even a feel to them as the hand moves across the

page. As you proofread, you can probably tell if a word doesn't look quite right. In such cases, the solution is obvious: Look the word up in the dictionary.

A word processor equipped with a spelling checker is a useful alternative to a dictionary, but only up to a point. A spelling checker will not tell you how to spell words not listed in its dictionary; nor will it help you catch words commonly confused, such as *accept* and *except*, or common typographical errors, such as *own* for *won*. You will still need to proofread, and for some words you may need to turn to the dictionary.

NOTE: To check for correct use of commonly confused words (*accept* and *except*, *its* and *it's*, and so on), consult section 31, the Glossary of Usage.

Major spelling rules. If you need to improve your spelling, review the following rules and exceptions.

1. Use *i* before *e* except after *c* or when sounded like *ay*, as in *neighbor* and *weigh*.

I BEFORE *E*	relieve, believe, sieve, niece, fierce, frieze
E BEFORE *I*	receive, deceive, sleigh, freight, eight
EXCEPTIONS	seize, either, weird, height, foreign, leisure

2. Generally, drop a final silent *e* when adding a suffix that begins with a vowel. Keep the final *e* if the suffix begins with a consonant.

desire, desiring	achieve, achievement
remove, removable	care, careful

Words such as *changeable*, *judgment*, *argument*, and *truly* are exceptions.

3. When adding *-s* or *-ed* to words ending in *y*, ordinarily change *y* to *i* when the *y* is preceded by a consonant but not when it is preceded by a vowel.

comedy, comedies	monkey, monkeys
dry, dried	play, played

With proper names ending in *y*, however, do not change the *y* to *i* even if it is preceded by a consonant: *the Dougherty family, the Doughertys*.

4. If a final consonant is preceded by a single vowel *and* the consonant ends a one-syllable word or a stressed syllable, double the consonant when adding a suffix beginning with a vowel.

bet, betting	occur, occurrence
commit, committed	

5. Add -*s* to form the plural of most nouns; add -*es* to singular nouns ending in -*s*, -*sh*, -*ch*, and -*x*.

table, tables	church, churches
paper, papers	dish, dishes

Ordinarily add -*s* to nouns ending in -*o* when the *o* is preceded by a vowel. Add -*es* when it is preceded by a consonant.

radio, radios	hero, heroes
video, videos	tomato, tomatoes

To form the plural of a hyphenated compound word, add the -*s* to the chief word even if it does not appear at the end.

mother-in-law, mothers-in-law

NOTE: English words derived from other languages such as Latin or French sometimes form the plural as they would in their original language.

medium, media	chateau, chateaux
criterion, criteria	

ESL NOTE: Spelling may vary slightly among English-speaking countries. This can prove particularly confusing for ESL students, who may have learned British or Canadian English. Following is a list of some common words spelled differently in American and British English. Consult a dictionary for others.

AMERICAN	**BRITISH**
canceled, traveled	cancelled, travelled
color, humor	colour, humour
judgment	judgement
check	cheque

AMERICAN	BRITISH
realize, apologize	realise, apologise
defense	defence
anemia, anesthetic	anaemia, anaesthetic
theater, center	theatre, centre
fetus	foetus
mold, smolder	mould, smoulder
civilization	civilisation
connection, inflection	connexion, inflexion
licorice	liquorice

Commonly misspelled words. One way to improve your spelling is to work with words that are commonly misspelled. Ask a friend to dictate the following words to you, make a list of any words you misspell, and then practice writing these words correctly.

absence	calendar	embarrass
academic	candidate	eminent
accidentally	cemetery	emphasize
accommodate	changeable	entirely
acknowledge	characteristic	environment
acquaintance	column	especially
acquire	commitment	exaggerated
across	committed	exhaust
address	committee	existence
all right	competitive	familiar
altogether	conceivable	fascinate
amateur	conferred	February
analyze	conscience	foreign
answer	conscious	forty
apparently	courteous	fourth
appearance	criticism	government
appropriate	curiosity	grammar
argument	dealt	guidance
arrangement	decision	harass
ascend	definitely	height
athlete	describe	illiterate
athletics	description	incidentally
attendance	desperate	incredible
audience	develop	indispensable
basically	disappear	inevitable
beginning	disappoint	intelligence
believe	disastrous	interesting
benefited	dissatisfied	irrelevant
bureau	eighth	irresistible
business	eligible	knowledge

laboratory	practically	secretary
license	precede	seize
loneliness	precedence	separate
maintenance	preference	sergeant
maneuver	preferred	similar
mathematics	prejudice	sincerely
mischievous	privilege	sophomore
necessary	proceed	subtly
noticeable	professor	succeed
occasionally	pronunciation	surprise
occurred	quiet	thorough
occurrence	quite	tragedy
omitted	quizzes	transferred
optimistic	receive	truly
pamphlet	recommend	unnecessarily
parallel	reference	usually
particularly	referred	vacuum
pastime	repetition	vengeance
perseverance	restaurant	villain
perspiration	rhythm	weird
phenomenon	ridiculous	whether
physically	roommate	writing
playwright	sandwich	
politics	schedule	

24b. The hyphen

In addition to the following guidelines, a dictionary will help you make decisions about hyphenation.

Compound words. The dictionary will tell you whether to treat a compound word as a hyphenated compound (*water-repellent*), one word (*waterproof*), or two words (*water table*). If the compound word is not in the dictionary, treat it as two words.

▶ The prosecutor chose not to cross—examine any
                                         ∧
   witnesses.

▶ Grandma kept a small note book in her apron pocket.

▶ Alice walked through the looking⁄glass into a backward

   world.

Words functioning together as an adjective. When two or more words function together as an adjective before a noun, connect them with a hyphen. Generally, do not use a hyphen when such compounds follow the noun.

▶ Pat Hobbs is not yet a well‿known candidate.

▶ After our television campaign, Pat Hobbs will be

 well╱known.

Do not use a hyphen to connect *-ly* adverbs to the words they modify.

▶ A slowly╱moving truck tied up traffic.

NOTE: In a series, hyphens are suspended: Do you prefer first-, second-, or third-class tickets?

Conventional uses. Hyphenate the written form of fractions and of compound numbers from twenty-one to ninety-nine. Also use the hyphen with the prefixes *all-*, *ex-*, and *self-* and with the suffix *-elect*.

▶ One‿fourth of my income goes for rent.

▶ The charity is funding more self‿help projects.

Division of a word at the end of a line. If a word must be divided at the end of a line, use these guidelines:

1. Divide words between syllables.
2. Never divide one-syllable words.
3. Never divide a word so that a single letter stands alone at the end of a line or fewer than three letters begin a line.
4. When dividing a compound word at the end of a line, either make the break between the words that form the compound or put the whole word on the next line.

DOCUMENTATION

Documentation

In academic research papers and in any other writing that borrows information from sources, the borrowed information must be clearly documented.

You should use the system of documentation recommended by your instructor. *A Pocket Style Manual* describes three systems: MLA style, used in English and the humanities; APA style, used in the social sciences; and footnotes or endnotes. See sections 27, 28, and 29. For other systems, consult the list of style manuals in section 30.

25. When to cite a source; avoiding plagiarism

In research writing, you document sources to let readers know where your information came from and to give credit to the writers whose words and ideas you have borrowed. To borrow another's words and ideas without proper acknowledgment is a form of dishonesty known as plagiarism.

To avoid plagiarism, you must cite all quotations, summaries, and paraphrases as well as any facts or ideas that are not common knowledge. In addition, you must be careful to put quotations in quotation marks and to express all paraphrases and summaries in your own words.

25a. Citing quotations

Quotations must be copied accurately, word for word, and they must be placed in quotation marks unless they have been formally set off from the text (see p. 88). The following example and other examples in this section are documented with the MLA style of in-text citation described in section 27.

According to Eugene Linden, "There is a good deal of evidence that maternal behavior in chimps is not entirely automatic" (93).

This citation has two parts: a signal phrase — *According to Eugene Linden* — and a page number in parentheses — (93). Readers interested in tracking down the source can turn to the list of works cited at the end of the paper, where full publishing information will be listed under the name *Linden*; once readers have located the source in the library, they can turn to the exact page on which the quotation appears.

25b. Citing summaries, paraphrases, facts, and ideas

A summary condenses information from a source, perhaps capsulizing a chapter in a paragraph or a paragraph in a single sentence. A paraphrase reports information in roughly the same number of words used by the source. Neither a summary nor a paraphrase borrows extensive language from a source.

ORIGINAL SOURCE

Public and scientific interest in the question of apes' ability to use language first soared some 15 years ago when Washoe, a chimpanzee raised like a human child by R. Allen Gardner and Beatrice Gardner of the University of Nevada, learned to make hand signs for many words and even seemed to be making short sentences.   —Eckholm, "Pygmy," p. B7

SUMMARY

Interest in the ability of apes to use language was sparked in the early seventies, when a chimpanzee named Washoe was taught sign language by R. Allen Gardner and Beatrice Gardner (Eckholm B7).

PARAPHRASE

Interest in the ability of apes to learn language mounted in the early seventies, with reports that Washoe, a chimpanzee raised and trained by professors R. Allen Gardner and Beatrice Gardner, had learned words in sign language and may even have created short sentences (Eckholm B7).

NOTE: In these examples, the MLA parenthetical citation includes the author's name because the author has not been named in a signal phrase.

In addition to citing summaries and paraphrases, cite any other specific borrowings from a source: statistics, little-known facts, controversial data, charts, graphs, diagrams, and original ideas. The only exception is common knowledge — information that readers could find in any number of general sources because it is commonly known. For example, the current population of the United States is common knowledge, as are the dates of the Civil War and the names of the astronauts who first landed on the moon.

As a rule, when you have seen certain facts repeatedly in your reading, you don't need to cite them. When they have appeared in only one or two sources or when they are controversial, however, you should cite them. When in doubt, cite the source.

25c. Avoiding plagiarism by putting summaries and paraphrases in your own words

When you summarize or paraphrase, it is not enough to name the source; you must restate the source's meaning using your own words. You are guilty of plagiarism if you borrow strings of words without using quotation marks or if you closely mimic an author's sentence structure. The following paraphrases are plagiarized — even though the source is cited — because their language is too close to that of the original source.

ORIGINAL VERSION
If the existence of a signing ape was unsettling for linguists, it was also startling news for animal behaviorists.   — Davis, *Eloquent Animals*, p. 26

UNACCEPTABLE BORROWING OF WORDS
The existence of a signing ape unsettled linguists and startled animal behaviorists (Davis 26).

UNACCEPTABLE BORROWING OF STRUCTURE
If the presence of a sign-language-using chimp was disturbing for scientists studying language, it was also surprising to scientists studying animal behavior (Davis 26).

To avoid plagiarizing an author's language, resist the temptation to look at the source while you are summarizing or paraphrasing. Close the book, write from memory, and then open the book to check for accuracy. This technique prevents you from being captivated by the words on the page.

ACCEPTABLE PARAPHRASES

When they learned of an ape's ability to use sign language, both linguists and animal behaviorists were taken by surprise (Davis 26).

According to Flora Davis, linguists and animal behaviorists were unprepared for the news that a chimp could communicate with its trainers through sign language (26).

26. How to integrate quotations

Readers should be able to move from your own words to the words you quote from a source without feeling a jolt.

26a. Using signal phrases

Avoid dropping quotations into the text without warning; instead, provide clear signal phrases, usually including the author's name, to prepare readers for the source.

DROPPED QUOTATION

Although the bald eagle is still listed as an endangered species, its ever-increasing population is very encouraging. "The bald eagle seems to have stabilized its population, at the very least, almost everywhere" (Sheppard 96).

QUOTATION WITH SIGNAL PHRASE

Although the bald eagle is still listed as an endangered species, its ever-increasing population is very encouraging. According to ornithologist Jay Sheppard, "The bald eagle seems to have stabi-

lized its population, at the very least, almost
everywhere" (96).

NOTE: The examples in this section are documented with
the MLA system of in-text citations (see section 27).

To avoid monotony, try to vary your signal phrases.
The following models suggest a range of possibilities.

> In the words of researcher Herbert Terrace, ". . ."
>
> As Flora Davis has noted, ". . ."
>
> The Gardners, Washoe's trainers, point out that ". . ."
>
> ". . . ," claims linguist Noam Chomsky.
>
> Psychologist H. S. Terrace offers an odd argument for
> this view: ". . ."
>
> Terrace answers these objections with the following
> analysis: ". . ."

When the signal phrase includes a verb, choose one
that is appropriate in the context. Is your source arguing
a point, making an observation, reporting a fact, drawing
a conclusion, refuting an argument, or stating a belief? By
choosing an appropriate verb, such as one on the following
list, you can make your source's stance clear.

admits	contends	reasons
agrees	declares	refutes
argues	denies	rejects
asserts	emphasizes	reports
believes	insists	responds
claims	notes	suggests
compares	observes	thinks
confirms	points out	writes

26b. Using the ellipsis mark and brackets

Two useful marks of punctuation, the ellipsis mark and
brackets, allow you to keep quoted material to a minimum
and to integrate it smoothly into your own text.

The ellipsis mark. To condense a quoted passage, you
can use the ellipsis mark (three periods, with spaces between) to indicate that you have omitted words. The sentence that remains must be grammatically complete.

In a recent <u>New York Times</u> article, Erik Eckholm
reports that "a 4-year-old pygmy chimpanzee . . .
has demonstrated what scientists say are the most
humanlike linguistic skills ever documented in another animal" (Al).

The writer has omitted the words *at a research center near
Atlanta*, which appeared in the original.

When you want to omit a full sentence or more, use
a period before the three ellipsis dots.

According to Wade, the horse Clever Hans "could
apparently count by tapping out numbers with his
hoof. . . . Clever Hans owes his celebrity to his
master's innocence. Von Osten sincerely believed
he had taught Hans to solve arithmetical
problems" (1349).

Ordinarily, do not use an ellipsis mark at the beginning or at the end of a quotation. Your readers will understand that the quoted material is taken from a longer
passage. The only exception occurs when you have omitted
words at the end of the final quoted sentence.

Brackets.   Brackets allow you to insert words of your
own into quoted material, perhaps to explain a confusing
reference or to keep a sentence grammatical in your context.

Robert Seyfarth writes that "Premack [a scientist
at the University of Pennsylvania] taught a seven-
year-old chimpanzee, Sarah, that the word for
'apple' was a small, plastic triangle" (13).

If your typewriter has no brackets, ink them in by hand.

26c. Setting off long quotations

When you quote more than four typed lines of prose or
more than three lines of poetry, set off the quotation by
indenting it ten spaces from the left margin. Use the normal right margin and do not single-space.

Long quotations should be introduced by an informative sentence, usually followed by a colon. Quotation marks are unnecessary because the indented format tells readers that the words are taken directly from the source.

Desmond describes how Washoe, when the Gardners returned her to an ape colony in Oklahoma, tried signing to the other apes:

> One particularly memorable day, a snake spread terror through the castaways on the ape island, and all but one fled in panic. This male sat absorbed, staring intently at the serpent. Then Washoe was seen running over signing to him "come, hurry up." (42)

Notice that in the MLA style of citation, the parenthetical citation at the end of an indented quotation goes outside the final period.

27. MLA documentation style

The Modern Language Association (MLA) recommends in-text citations that refer readers to a list of works cited.

27a. MLA in-text citations

An MLA in-text citation is made with a combination of a signal phrase and a parenthetical reference. The signal phrase usually names the author of the source; the parenthetical reference includes at least a page number.

Author in signal phrase, page number in parentheses. If you can name the author in a signal phrase, you can keep the information in parentheses brief. Usually only a page number is required.

Flora Davis reports that a chimp at the Yerkes Primate Research Center "has combined words into new sentences that she was never taught" (67).

The signal phrase — *Flora Davis reports* — provides the name of the author; the parenthetical citation gives the page number where the quoted sentence may be found. By looking up the author's last name in the list of works cited, readers will find complete information about the work's title, publisher, and date of publication.

Author and page number in parentheses.   If the signal phrase does not include the author's name (or if there is no signal phrase), the author's last name must appear in parentheses with the page number.

Although the baby chimp lived only a few hours,

Washoe signed to it before it died (Davis 42).

Multiple authors.   When a source has two or three authors, either name all the authors in a signal phrase or include their last names in the parenthetical reference: (Polk, Jones, and Walker 25). When a source has four or more authors, use the name of the first author followed by "et al." (Latin for "and others") in the signal phrase or in the parentheses: (Hare et al. 36).

Unknown author.   If an author is not given, either mention the full title in a signal phrase or use a short form of the title in the parentheses: ("Talking" 89). "Talking" is a short title of the unsigned newspaper article "Talking with Chimpanzees."

Two or more works by the same author.   If your list of works cited includes more than one work by the same author, either mention the full title of the work in the signal phrase or use a short form of the title in the parentheses. Titles or short titles of books are underlined: (El-oquent 67). Titles or short titles of articles are put in quotation marks: ("Talking" 89).

If you have not used the author's name in a signal phrase, include it in the parentheses: (Davis, Eloquent 67).

Work in an anthology.   Put the name of the author of the work (not the editor of the anthology) in the signal phrase or in the parentheses.

A novel, play, or poem.   Include information that will enable readers to find the passage in various editions of the work. For a novel, put the page number first and then, if possible, indicate the part or chapter in which the passage can be found: (56; ch. 3). For a verse play, list the act, scene, and line numbers: (3.2.21–23). For a poem, cite the part (if there are a number of parts) and the line numbers: (10.209–11).

Multivolume work. If your paper cites more than one volume of a multivolume work, you must indicate in the parentheses which volume you are referring to: (Graves 2: 279).

Indirect source. When a writer or speaker's quoted words appear in a work written by another author, use the abbreviation "qtd. in" before the author's name in the parenthetical reference: (qtd. in Toner 24).

27b. MLA list of works cited

An alphabetized list of works cited, which appears at the end of your paper, gives full publishing information for each of the sources you have cited in the paper. For advice on constructing the list, see page 97. A sample list of works cited appears on page 98.

The following models illustrate the MLA form for entries in the list of works cited.

Books

BASIC FORMAT FOR A BOOK
For most books, arrange the information into three units, each followed by a period: (1) the author's name, last name first; (2) the title and subtitle, underlined; and (3) the place of publication, the publisher, and the date.

McPherson, James M. <u>Battle Cry of Freedom: The Civil War Era</u>. New York: Oxford UP, 1988.

TWO OR THREE AUTHORS
Miller, Kenton, and Laura Tangley. <u>Trees of Life: Saving Tropical Forests and Their Biological Wealth</u>. Boston: Beacon, 1991.

FOUR OR MORE AUTHORS
Medhurst, Martin J., et al. <u>Cold War Rhetoric: Strategy, Metaphor, and Ideology</u>. New York: Greenwood, 1990.

UNKNOWN AUTHOR

The Times Atlas of the World.   8th ed. New York:

New York Times, 1990.

CORPORATE AUTHOR

Fidelity Investments.   Mutual Fund Services Hand-

book.   Boston: Fidelity Investments, 1991.

EDITOR

Dubus, Andre, ed.   Into the Silence: American

Stories.   Cambridge: Green Street, 1988.

AUTHOR WITH AN EDITOR

Franklin, Benjamin.   The Autobiography and Other

Writings.   Ed. Kenneth Silverman.   New York:

Penguin, 1986.

TRANSLATION

Eco, Umberto.   Foucault's Pendulum.   Trans.

William Weaver.   San Diego: Harcourt, 1989.

TWO OR MORE WORKS BY THE SAME AUTHOR

Tan, Amy.   The Joy Luck Club.   New York: Put-

nam's, 1989.

---.   The Kitchen God's Wife.   New York: Put-

nam's, 1991.

EDITION OTHER THAN THE FIRST

Lindemann, Erika.   A Rhetoric for Writing Teach-

ers.   2nd ed.   New York: Oxford UP, 1987.

MULTIVOLUME WORK

Foote, Shelby.   The Civil War: A Narrative.

3 vols.   New York: Random, 1958—74.

WORK IN AN ANTHOLOGY

Bambara, Toni Cade.   "My Man Bovanne."   Breaking

Ice: An Anthology of Contemporary Afro-

American Fiction.   Ed. Terry McMillan.   New

York: Penguin, 1990.   33—38.

INTRODUCTION OR PREFACE

Van Vechten, Carl. Introduction. <u>Last Operas
    and Plays</u>. By Gertrude Stein. Ed. Van
    Vechten. New York: Vintage-Random, 1975.
    vii-xix.

UNSIGNED ENCYCLOPEDIA ARTICLE

"Croatia-Slavonia." <u>Encyclopaedia Britannica</u>.
    11th ed. 1910.

Periodicals

ARTICLE IN A MONTHLY MAGAZINE

Baker, Kenneth. "When the Nazis Took Aim at Mod-
    ern Art." <u>Smithsonian</u> July 1991: 86–95.

ARTICLE IN A WEEKLY MAGAZINE

Gorman, Christine. "The Fight over Food Labels."
    <u>Time</u> 15 July 1991: 52–56.

ARTICLE IN A NEWSPAPER

Gladwell, Malcolm. "The Subtler Shades of Rac-
    ism." <u>Washington Post</u> 15 July 1991: A3.

ARTICLE IN A JOURNAL PAGINATED BY VOLUME

Segal, Gabriel. "Seeing What Is Not There."
    <u>Philosophical Review</u> 98 (1989): 189–214.

ARTICLE IN A JOURNAL PAGINATED BY ISSUE

Johnson, G. J. "A Distinctiveness Model of Ser-
    ial Learning." <u>Psychological Review</u> 98.2
    (1991): 204–17.

UNSIGNED PERIODICAL ARTICLE

"When Ballots Turn toward Mecca." <u>U. S. News and
    World Report</u> 25 June 1990: 17–18.

REVIEW

Donoghue, Denis. "A Worldly Philosopher." Rev.
    of <u>The Examined Life</u>, by Robert Nozick.
    <u>Wilson Quarterly</u> 14.2 (1990): 92–94.

EDITORIAL

"A Farm-Water Utility." Editorial. <u>Miami Herald</u>
19 June 1990: 10A.

LETTER TO THE EDITOR

Daley, Dan, and Sheila Daley. Letter. <u>Common-
weal</u> 15 June 1990: 370.

Other sources

MATERIAL FROM A DATABASE

Horn, Pamela. "The Victorian Governess." <u>His-
tory of Education</u> 18 (1989): 333–44. ERIC
EJ 401 533.

PAMPHLET OR GOVERNMENT PUBLICATION

United States. Dept. of the Interior. National
Park Service. <u>Ford's Theatre and the House
Where Lincoln Died</u>. Washington: GPO, 1989.

DISSERTATION

Fedorko, Kathy Anne. "Edith Wharton's Haunted
House: The Gothic in Her Fiction." Diss.
Rutgers U, 1987.

DISSERTATION ABSTRACT

Berkman, Anne Elizabeth. "The Quest for Authenticity: The Novels of Toni Morrison." <u>DAI</u>
48 (1988): 2059A. Columbia U.

PERSONAL INTERVIEW

Shaw, Lloyd. Personal interview. 21 Mar. 1992.

PUBLISHED INTERVIEW

Francis, Dick. Interview. <u>Writer</u> July 1990:
9–10.

COMPUTER SOFTWARE

<u>When in Time Is Carmen Sandiego?</u> Computer soft-
ware. Brøderbund, 1989. IBM/Tandy, disk.

FILM

North by Northwest. Dir. Alfred Hitchcock. MGM,

1959.

TELEVISION PROGRAM

"Mr. Sears' Catalogue." The American Experience.

Narr. David McCullough. PBS. WGBH, Boston.

7 Aug. 1990.

LIVE PERFORMANCE OF A PLAY

As You Like It. By William Shakespeare. Dir.

Michael Kahn. The Shakespeare Theater,

Washington, DC. 29 May 1992.

RECORDING

Handel, George Frederick. Messiah. Cond.

Charles Mackerras. English Chamber Orch.

and the Ambrosian Singers. Angel, R 67-

2682, 1967.

27c. MLA information notes

Writers who use the MLA system of in-text citations may also use information notes for one of two purposes:

1. to provide additional information that might interrupt the flow of the paper yet is important enough to include;
2. to refer readers to sources not included in the list of works cited.

Information notes may be either footnotes or end-notes. Footnotes appear at the bottom of the page; end-notes appear at the end of the paper, just before the list of works cited. For either style, the notes are numbered consecutively throughout the paper. The text of the paper contains a raised arabic numeral that corresponds to the number of the note.

TEXT

There is still skepticism about whether the apes

merely imitate or respond to the cues of their

trainers.[1]

NOTE
[1] For a discussion of this issue, see Thomas A.
Sebeok and Jean Umiker-Sebeok, "Performing Animals: Secrets of the Trade," <u>Psychology Today</u> Nov.
1979: 78–91.

Information notes should not be confused with notes used
as an alternative to in-text citations. (See section 29.)

27d. MLA manuscript format

The Modern Language Association makes the following
recommendations about manuscript format.

Title and identification.   A title page is not necessary.
Unless instructed otherwise, against the left margin about
one inch from the top of the paper, place your name, the
instructor's name, the course name and number, and the
date on separate lines. Double-space between lines.

   Double-space after the heading and center the title of
the paper in the width of the page. Then double-space
again and begin typing the text of the paper.

Margins, spacing, and indentation.   Leave margins of
at least one inch but no more than an inch and a half at
the top, bottom, and sides of the page.

   Double-space between lines and indent the first line
of each paragraph five spaces from the left margin.

   For quotations longer than four typed lines of prose
or longer than three lines of verse, indent each line ten
spaces from the left margin. Double-space between the
body of the paper and the quotation, and double-space the
lines of the quotation.

Pagination.   Using arabic numerals, number all pages
at the upper right corner, one-half inch below the top edge.
Put your last name before each page number for clear
identification in case pages are misplaced.

Punctuation and typing.   In typing the paper, leave one
space after words, commas, colons, and semicolons and
between the dots in ellipses. Leave two spaces after periods, question marks, and exclamation points. To form a
dash, type two hyphens with no space between them; do
not put a space on either side of a dash.

Preparing the "Works Cited" page

On page 98 is a sample list of works cited. The list of works cited appears at the end of the paper.

To construct such a list, begin on a new page and title your list "Works Cited." Alphabetize the list by the last names of the authors (or editors); if a work has no author or editor, alphabetize by the first word of the title other than *a*, *an*, or *the*.

If two or more works by the same author appear in the list, use the author's name only for the first entry. For subsequent entries, use three hyphens followed by a period. List the titles in alphabetical order.

Do not indent the first line of each entry in the list but indent any additional lines five spaces. Double-space throughout.

NOTE: The sample "Works Cited" page shows you how to type your list of works cited. For information about the exact format of each entry in the list of works cited, consult the models on pages 91–95.

Works Cited

Bower, Bruce. "Kanzi Extends His Speech Reach." Science News 27 Aug. 1988: 140.

Crail, Ted. Apetalk and Whalespeak. Los Angeles: Tarcher, 1981.

Davis, Flora. Eloquent Animals: A Study in Animal Communication. New York: Coward, 1978.

Eckholm, Erik. "Kanzi the Chimp: A Life in Science," New York Times 25 June 1985, local ed.: C1+.

---. "Pygmy Chimp Readily Learns Language Skill." New York Times 24 June 1985, local ed.: A1+.

Patterson, Francine, and Eugene Linden. The Education of Koko. New York: Holt, 1981.

Savage-Rumbaugh, Sue, et al. "Spontaneous Symbol Acquisition and Communicative Use by Pygmy Chimpanzees (Pan paniscus)." Journal of Experimental Psychology 115 (1986): 211–35.

Seyfarth, Robert M. "Talking with Monkeys and Great Apes." International Wildlife Mar.–Apr. 1982: 13–18.

Terrace, H. S. Nim. New York: Knopf, 1979.

Terrace, H. S., et al. "Can an Ape Create a Sentence?" Science 206 (1979): 891–902.

28. APA documentation style

The American Psychological Association (APA) recommends in-text citations that refer readers to a list of references.

28a. APA in-text citations

The APA's in-text citations provide at least the author's last name and the date of publication. For direct quotations, a page number is given as well.

A quotation. Ordinarily, introduce the quotation with a signal phrase that includes the author's last name followed by the date of publication in parentheses. Put the page number in parentheses at the end of the quotation.

```
As Davis (1978) reports, "If the existence of a
signing ape was unsettling for linguists, it was
also startling news for animal behaviorists"
(p. 26).
```

When the author's name does not appear in the signal phrase, place the author's last name, the date, and the page number in parentheses at the end: (Davis, 1978, p. 26).

A summary or a paraphrase. For a summary or a paraphrase, include the author's last name and the date either in a signal phrase or in parentheses at the end. A page number is not required.

```
According to Davis (1978), when they learned of an
ape's ability to use sign language, both linguists
and animal behaviorists were taken by surprise.
```

```
When they learned of an ape's ability to use sign
language, both linguists and animal behaviorists
were taken by surprise (Davis, 1978).
```

Two authors. Name both authors in the signal phrase or parentheses each time you cite the work. In the parentheses, use "&" between the authors' names: (Patterson & Linden, 1981). In the signal phrase, use "and."

Three to five authors.   Identify all authors in the signal phrase or parentheses the first time you cite the source: (Caplow, Bahr, Chadwick, Hill, & Williamson, 1982). In subsequent citations, use the first author's name followed by "et al." in either the signal phrase or parentheses: (Caplow et al., 1982).

Six or more authors.   Use only the first author's name followed by "et al." in all citations: (Berger et al., 1971).

Unknown author.   If the author is not given, either use the complete title in a signal phrase or use the first two or three words of the title in the parenthetical citation: ("Strange Encounter," 1987). Titles of articles appear in quotation marks; titles of books are underlined.

If "Anonymous" is specified as the author, treat it as if it were a real name: (Anonymous, 1991). In the list of references, also use the name *Anonymous* as the author.

Two or more works in the same parentheses.   When your parenthetical citation names two or more works, put them in the same order that they appear in the list of references, separated by semicolons: (Berger et al., 1971; Smith, 1992).

Authors with the same last name.   To avoid confusion, use initials with the last names if your list of references contains two or more authors with the same last name: (J. A. Smith, 1992).

Personal communication.   Conversations, memos, letters, and similar unpublished person-to-person communications should be cited by initials, last name, and precise date: (L. Smith, personal communication, October 12, 1992). Do not include personal communications in the list of references.

28b. APA references

In APA style, the alphabetical list of works cited is entitled "References." Following are models illustrating the form that APA recommends for entries in the list of references. Observe all details: capitalization, punctuation, underlining, and so on. For explanations of these matters and for a sample "References" page, see pages 104–06.

Books

BASIC FORMAT FOR A BOOK
Linden, E. (1986). Silent partners: The legacy of the ape language experiments. New York: Random House.

TWO OR MORE AUTHORS
Patterson, F., & Linden, E. (1981). The education of Koko. New York: Holt, Rinehart and Winston.

CORPORATE AUTHOR
National Institute of Mental Health. (1976). Behavior modification: Perspective on a current issue. Rockville, MD: Author.

UNKNOWN AUTHOR
The Times atlas of the world. (1990). New York: New York Times.

EDITORS
Sebeok, T. A., & Umiker-Sebeok, D. J. (Eds.). (1980). Speaking of apes: A critical anthology of two-way communication with man. New York: Plenum Press.

TRANSLATION
Miller, A. (1990). The untouched key: Tracing childhood trauma in creativity and destructiveness (H. and H. Hannum, Trans.). New York: Doubleday.

EDITION OTHER THAN THE FIRST
Falk, J. S. (1978). Linguistics and language: A survey of basic concepts and implications (2nd ed.). New York: Wiley.

WORK IN AN ANTHOLOGY

Basso, K. H. (1970).   Silence in western Apache
    culture.   In P. Giglioli (Ed.), Language and
    social context (pp. 67—86).   Harmondsworth,
    England: Penguin.

Periodicals

ARTICLE IN A MAGAZINE

Seyfarth, R. M. (1982, March—April).   Talking
    with monkeys and great apes.   International
    Wildlife, pp. 13—18.

ARTICLE IN A NEWSPAPER

Cohen, D. L. (1990, June 20).   Counselors in ele-
    mentary schools: Children's "prevention spe-
    cialists."   Education Week, pp. 1, 14—16.

ARTICLE IN A JOURNAL PAGINATED BY VOLUME

Otto, M. L. (1984).   Child abuse: Group treatment
    for parents.   Personnel and Guidance Journal,
    62, 336—338.

ARTICLE IN A JOURNAL PAGINATED BY ISSUE

Nichols, R. G. (1986).   Word processing and basic
    writers.   Journal of Basic Writing,   5(2),
    81—97.

UNSIGNED ARTICLE IN A PERIODICAL

Help in fighting the war on drugs. (1990).   Chil-
    dren Today, 19(2), 2—3.

REVIEW

Crosby, F. (1990).   [Review of Equity and gender:
    The comparable worth debate].   Psychology of
    Women Quarterly, 14, 147—148.

LETTER TO THE EDITOR

Hopi, M., & Young, J. (1990).   European policies

serve to prevent homelessness [Letter to the
editor]. Public Welfare, 48(1), pp. 5–6.

Other sources

MATERIAL FROM A DATABASE

Seefeldt, R. W., & Lyon, M. A. (1990, March).
Personality characteristics of adult children
of alcoholics: Fact or fiction? Paper pre-
sented at the annual meeting of the American
Association for Counseling and Development,
Cincinnati, OH. (ERIC Document Reproduction
Service No. ED 316 784)

GOVERNMENT DOCUMENT

U.S. Department of State. (1986). Report to
Congress on voting practices in the United
Nations. Washington, DC: U.S. Government
Printing Office.

DISSERTATION ABSTRACT

Pellman, J. L. (1988). Community integration: Its
influence on the stresses of widowhood (Doc-
toral dissertation, University of Missouri,
1988). Dissertation Abstracts International,
49, 2367.

PROCEEDINGS OF CONFERENCE

Waterhouse, L. H. (1982). Maternal speech patterns
and differential development. In C. E. Johnson & C. L. Thew (Eds.), Proceedings of the
Second Annual International Congress for the
Study of Child Language (pp. 442–454). Washington, DC: University Press of America.

COMPUTER PROGRAM

When in time is Carmen Sandiego? (1989). San
Rafael, CA: Brøderbund Software, Inc.

VIDEOTAPE

Minasian, S. M. (Producer). (1985). <u>World of the</u>
<u>sea otter</u> [Videotape]. San Francisco: Marine
Mammal Fund.

Preparing the "References" page

On page 106 is a sample list of references in the APA
style. This list, titled "References," appears on a separate
page at the end of the paper.

A short form of the title of the paper appears in the
upper right-hand corner, above the page number. The
heading "References" is centered, and each entry in the
list begins at the left margin. Any additional lines in an
entry are indented three spaces. Double-spacing is used
throughout.

Alphabetizing the list. Alphabetize your list by the last
names of the authors (or editors); when the author or editor is unknown, alphabetize by the first word of the title
other than *a*, *an*, and *the*.

If your list includes two or more works by the same
author, arrange the entries by date, the earliest first. If
your list includes two or more articles by the same author
in the same year, arrange them alphabetically by title. Add
lowercase letters beginning with "a," "b," and so on,
within the parentheses immediately following the year:
(1992a, July 7).

Authors and dates. Invert all authors' names and use
initials instead of first names. With two or more authors,
use an ampersand (&). Use all authors' names; do not use
"et al."

After the names of the authors, place the date in
parentheses.

Titles of books and articles. Underline the titles and
subtitles of books; capitalize only the first word of the title
and subtitle (as well as all proper nouns).

Do not place titles of articles in quotation marks, and
capitalize only the first word of the title and subtitle (and
all proper nouns). Capitalize names of periodicals as you
would capitalize them ordinarily. (See section 22.)

The abbreviation "p." (or "pp.").   Abbreviations for "page" or "pages" are used before page numbers of magazine and newspaper articles and works in anthologies but not before page numbers of articles appearing in scholarly journals.

NOTE: The sample "References" page shows you how to type your list of references. For information about the exact format of each entry in your list, consult the models on pages 100−04.

References

Bower, B. (1988). Kanzi extends his speech
    reach. Science News, 134, 140.

Crail, T. (1981). Apetalk and whalespeak. Los
    Angeles: Tarcher.

Davis, F. (1978). Eloquent animals: A study in
    animal communication. New York: Coward,
    McCann & Geoghegan.

Eckholm, E. (1985a, June 25). Kanzi the chimp: A
    life in science. The New York Times, pp. C1,
    C3.

Eckholm, E. (1985b, June 24). Pygmy chimp read-
    ily learns language skill. The New York
    Times, pp. A1, B7.

Patterson, F., & Linden, E. (1981). The educa-
    tion of Koko. New York: Holt, Rinehart and
    Winston.

Savage-Rumbaugh, S., McDonald, K., Sevcik, R. A.,
    Hopkins, W. D., & Rubert, E. (1986). Sponta-
    neous acquisition and communicative use by
    champanzees (Pan paniscus). Journal of Exper-
    imental Psychology, 115, 211–213.

Seyfarth, R. M. (1982, March–April). Talking
    with monkeys and great apes. International
    Wildlife, pp. 13–18.

Terrace, H. W. (1979). Nim. New York: Knopf.

29. Footnotes or endnotes

Professors in some disciplines prefer traditional footnotes or endnotes to the in-text citations discussed in sections 27 and 28. Notes provide complete publishing information, either at the bottom of the page (footnotes) or at the end of the paper (endnotes). A raised arabic numeral in the text indicates that a quotation, paraphrase, or summary has been borrowed from a source; to find the publishing information for that source, readers consult the footnote or endnote with the corresponding number. Notes are numbered consecutively throughout the paper.

TEXT

For instance, Lana once described a cucumber as "banana which-is green."[9]

NOTE

  [9] Flora Davis, <u>Eloquent Animals: A Study in Animal Communication</u> (New York: Coward, 1978) 300.

29a. First reference to a source

The first time you cite a source in your paper, the note should include the full publishing information for that work as well as the page number of the specific quotation, paraphrase, or summary. The following models, which are consistent with the Modern Language Association's recommendations for notes, cover the formats that are most frequently encountered.

Books

BASIC FORMAT FOR A BOOK

  [1] James M. McPherson, <u>Battle Cry of Freedom: The Civil War Era</u> (New York: Oxford UP, 1988) 87.

TWO OR MORE AUTHORS

  [2] Kenton Miller and Laura Tangley, <u>Trees of Life: Saving Tropical Forests and Their Biological Wealth</u> (Boston: Beacon, 1991) 17.

UNKNOWN AUTHOR
    [3] The Times Atlas of the World, 8th ed. (New York: New York Times, 1990) 95.

EDITORS
    [4] Andre Dubus, ed., Into the Silence: American Stories (Cambridge: Green Street, 1988) 3–4.

TRANSLATION
    [5] Umberto Eco, Foucault's Pendulum, trans. William Weaver (San Diego: Harcourt, 1989) 151.

EDITION OTHER THAN THE FIRST
    [6] Erika Lindemann, A Rhetoric for Writing Teachers, 2nd ed. (New York: Oxford UP, 1987) 146.

MULTIVOLUME WORK
    [7] Shelby Foote, The Civil War: A Narrative, vol. 2 (New York: Random, 1963) 459.

WORK IN AN ANTHOLOGY
    [8] Toni Cade Bambara, "My Man Bovanne," Breaking Ice: An Anthology of Contemporary Afro-American Fiction, ed. Terry McMillan (New York: Penguin, 1990) 33.

ENCYCLOPEDIA OR DICTIONARY
    [9] "Croatia-Slavonia," Encyclopaedia Britannica, 1910 ed.

Periodicals

ARTICLE IN A MAGAZINE
    [10] Kenneth Baker, "When the Nazis Took Aim at Modern Art," Smithsonian July 1991: 93.

ARTICLE IN A NEWSPAPER
    [11] Malcolm Gladwell, "The Subtler Shades of Racism," Washington Post 15 July 1991: A3.

ARTICLE IN A JOURNAL PAGINATED BY VOLUME
[12] Gabriel Segal, "Seeing What Is Not There," Philosophical Review 98 (1989): 201.

ARTICLE IN A JOURNAL PAGINATED BY ISSUE
[13] G. J. Johnson, "A Distinctiveness Model of Serial Learning," Psychological Review 98.2 (1991): 215.

UNSIGNED PERIODICAL ARTICLE
[14] "When Ballots Turn Toward Mecca," U.S. News and World Report 25 June 1990: 17.

REVIEW
[15] Denis Donoghue, "A Worldly Philosopher," rev. of The Examined Life, by Robert Nozick, Wilson Quarterly 14.2 (1990): 92.

Other sources

MATERIAL FROM A DATABASE
[16] Pamela Horn, "The Victorian Governess," History of Education 18 (1989) 336 (ERIC EJ 401 533).

PAMPHLET OR GOVERNMENT PUBLICATION
[17] United States, Dept. of the Interior, National Park Service, Ford's Theatre and the House Where Lincoln Died (Washington: GPO, 1989) 1.

DISSERTATION
[18] Kathy Anne Fedorko, "Edith Wharton's Haunted House: The Gothic in Her Fiction," diss., Rutgers U, 1987, 59.

DISSERTATION ABSTRACT
[19] Anne Elizabeth Berkman, "The Quest for Authenticity: The Novels of Toni Morrison," DAI 48 (1988): 2059A (Columbia U).

PERSONAL INTERVIEW

    [20] Lloyd Shaw, personal interview, 16 May 1992.

29b. Subsequent references to a source

Subsequent references to a work that has already been cited in a note should be given in shortened form. You need to give only enough information so that the reader can identify which work you are referring to — usually the author's last name and a page number. The abbreviations *ibid.* and *op. cit.* are no longer used.

    [21] Linden 129.

    [22] Fisher and Ury 16.

If you are using more than one work by one author or two works by authors with the same last name, cite the author's last name and a shortened title.

    [23] Linden, <u>Silent</u> 53.

    [24] Linden, <u>Apes</u> 136.

When you use notes as your method of documentation, you may not need a list of works cited, since complete publishing information is given in the notes themselves. Some professors prefer, however, that you include an alphabetized list of the works cited in the paper or a bibliography of the works you consulted, whether or not they were cited. If you do include a list of works cited or a bibliography, use the MLA style described on pages 91–95.

30. A list of style manuals

A Pocket Style Manual describes three commonly used systems of documentation: MLA style, used in English and the humanities (see section 27); APA style, used in psychology and the social sciences (see section 28); and footnotes and endnotes (see section 29). Following is a list of style manuals used in a variety of disciplines.

BIOLOGY

Council of Biology Editors. *CBE Style Manual: A Guide for Authors, Editors, and Publishers in the Biological Sciences.* 5th ed. Bethesda: Council of Biology Editors, 1983.

CHEMISTRY

American Chemical Society. *American Chemical Society Style Guide: A Manual for Authors and Editors.* 2nd ed. Washington: American Chemical Society Publishing, 1986.

ENGLISH AND THE HUMANITIES

Gibaldi, Joseph, and Walter S. Achtert. *MLA Handbook for Writers of Research Papers.* 3rd ed. New York: Modern Language Assn. of America, 1988.

GEOLOGY

Bates, Robert L., Rex Buchanan, and Marla Adkins-Heljeson, eds. *Geowriting: A Guide to Writing, Editing, and Printing in Earth Science.* 5th ed. Alexandria: American Geological Inst., 1992.

LAW

Columbia Law Review. *A Uniform System of Citation.* 15th ed. Cambridge: Harvard Law Review, 1991.

LINGUISTICS

Linguistic Society of America. "LSA Style Sheet." Published annually in the December issue of the *LSA Bulletin.*

MATHEMATICS

American Mathematical Society. *A Manual for Authors of Mathematical Papers.* 8th ed. Providence: American Mathematical Society, 1984.

MEDICINE

International Steering Committee of Medical Editors. "Uniform Requirements for Manuscripts Submitted to Biomedical Journals." *Annals of Internal Medicine* 90 (Jan. 1979): 95–99.

PHYSICS

American Institute of Physics. *Style Manual for Guidance in the Preparation of Papers.* 4th ed. New York: American Inst. of Physics, 1990.

PSYCHOLOGY AND THE SOCIAL SCIENCES

American Psychological Association. *Publication Manual of the American Psychological Association* 3rd ed. Washington: American Psychological Assn., 1983.

GLOSSARIES

Glossary of usage
Glossary of grammatical terms

31. Glossary of usage

This glossary includes words commonly confused, words commonly misused, and words that are nonstandard. It also lists colloquialisms that may be appropriate in informal speech but are inappropriate in formal writing.

a, an Use *an* before a vowel sound, *a* before a consonant sound: *an apple, a peach.* In words beginning with *h*, if the *h* is silent, the word begins with a vowel sound: *an hour, an honorable deed.* If the *h* is pronounced, the word begins with a consonant sound: *a hospital, a hymn.*

accept, except *Accept* is a verb meaning "to receive." *Except* is usually a preposition meaning "excluding": I will *accept* all the packages *except* that one. *Except* is also a verb meaning "to exclude": Please *except* that item from the list.

advice, advise *Advice* is a noun, *advise* a verb: We *advise* you to follow John's *advice.*

affect, effect *Affect* is usually a verb meaning "to influence." *Effect* is usually a noun meaning "result": The drug did not *affect* the disease, and it had several adverse side *effects.* *Effect* can also be a verb meaning "to bring about": Only the president can *effect* such a dramatic change.

all ready, already *All ready* means "completely prepared." *Already* means "previously": Susan was *all ready* for the concert, but her friends had *already* left.

all right *All right* is always written as two words. *Alright* is nonstandard.

all together, altogether *All together* means "everyone gathered." *Altogether* means "entirely": We were not *altogether* certain that we could bring the family *all together* for the reunion.

allusion, illusion An *allusion* is an indirect reference, an *illusion* is a misconception or false impression: Did you catch my *allusion* to Shakespeare? Mirrors give the room an *illusion* of depth.

a lot *A lot* is two words. Do not write *alot.*

among, between Ordinarily, use *among* with three or more entities, *between* with two: The prize was divided *among* several contestants. You have a choice *between* carrots and beans.

amount, number   Use *amount* with quantities that cannot be counted; use *number* with those that can: This recipe calls for a large *amount* of sugar. We have a large *number* of toads in our garden.

an   See *a, an*.

and/or   Avoid *and/or* except in technical or legal documents.

anxious   *Anxious* means "worried" or "apprehensive." In formal writing, avoid using *anxious* to mean "eager": We are *eager* [not *anxious*] to see your new house.

anyone, any one   *Anyone*, an indefinite pronoun, means "any person at all." *Any one* refers to a particular person or thing in a group: *Anyone* from Chicago may choose *any one* of the games on display.

anyways, anywheres   *Anyways* and *anywheres* are nonstandard for *anyway* and *anywhere*.

as   *As* is sometimes used to mean "because." But do not use it if there is any chance of ambiguity: We canceled the picnic *because* [not *as*] it began raining. An *as* here could mean "because" or "when."

as, like   See *like, as*.

awful   The adjective *awful* means "awe-inspiring." Colloquially it is used to mean "terrible" or "bad." The adverb *awfully* is sometimes used in conversation as an intensifier meaning "very." In formal writing, avoid these colloquial uses: I was *very* [not *awfully*] upset last night.

awhile, a while   *Awhile* is an adverb; it can modify a verb, but it cannot be the object of a preposition such as *for*. The two-word form *a while* is a noun preceded by an article and therefore can be the object of a preposition. Stay *awhile*. Stay for *a while*.

bad, badly   *Bad* is an adjective, *badly* an adverb: They felt *bad* about being early and ruining the surprise. Her arm hurt *badly* after she slid into second. (See section 13.)

being as, being that   *Being* as and *being that* are nonstandard expressions. Write *because* or *since* instead.

beside, besides   *Beside* is a preposition meaning "at the side of" or "next to": Annie Oakley slept with her gun *beside* her bed. *Besides* is a preposition meaning "except" or "in addition to": No one *besides* Terrie can have that ice cream. *Besides* is also an adverb meaning "in addition": I'm not hungry; *besides*, I don't like ice cream.

between   See *among, between*.

bring, take   Use *bring* when an object is being transported toward you, *take* when it is being moved away: Please *bring* me a glass of water. Please *take* these magazines to Mr. Scott.

burst, bursted; bust, busted   *Burst* is an irregular verb meaning "to come open or fly apart suddenly or violently." The past-tense form *bursted* is nonstandard. *Bust* and *busted* are slang for *burst* and, along with *bursted*, should not be used in formal writing.

can, may   *Can* is traditionally reserved for ability, *may* for permission: *Can* you ski down the advanced slope without falling? *May* I help you?

capital, capitol   *Capital* refers to a city, *capitol* to a building where lawmakers meet: The residents of the state *capital* protested the development plans. The *capitol* has undergone extensive renovations. *Capital* also refers to wealth or resources.

cite, site   *Cite* means "to quote as an authority or example." *Site* is usually a noun meaning "a particular place": He *cited* the zoning law in his argument against the proposed *site* of the gas station.

coarse, course   *Coarse* means "crude" or "rough in texture": The *coarse* weave of the wall hanging gave it a three-dimensional quality. *Course* usually refers to a path, a playing field, or a unit of study; the expression *of course* means "certainly": I plan to take a *course* in car repair this summer. *Of course*, you are welcome to join me.

complement, compliment   *Complement* is a verb meaning "to go with or complete" or a noun meaning "something that completes." *Compliment* as a verb means "to flatter"; as a noun it means "flattering remark": Her skill at rushing the net *complements* his skill at volleying. Jill's music arrangements receive many *compliments*.

conscience, conscious   *Conscience* is a noun meaning "moral principles"; *conscious* is an adjective meaning "aware or alert": Let your *conscience* be your guide. Were you *conscious* of his love for you?

continual, continuous   *Continual* means "repeated regularly and frequently": She grew weary of the *continual* telephone calls. *Continuous* means "extended or prolonged without interruption": The broken siren made a *continuous* wail.

could care less   *Could care less* is a nonstandard expression. Write *couldn't care less* instead.

could of   *Could of* is nonstandard for *could have*.

criteria   *Criteria* is the plural of *criterion*, which means "a standard, rule, or test on which a judgment or decision can be based": The only *criterion* for the job is a willingness to work overtime.

data   *Data* is the plural of *datum*, which means "a fact or proposition." Many writers now treat *data* as singular or plural depending on the meaning of the sentence. Some experts insist, however, that *data* can only be plural: The new *data suggest* [not *suggests*] that our theory is correct. The singular form *datum* is rarely used.

different from, different than   Ordinarily, write *different from*: Your sense of style is *different from* Jim's. However, *different than* is acceptable to avoid an awkward construction: Please let me know if your plans are *different than* [to avoid *from what*] they were six weeks ago.

don't   *Don't* is the contraction for *do not*: I *don't* want any. *Don't* should not be used as the contraction for *does not*, which is *doesn't*: He *doesn't* [not *don't*] want any.

double negative   Standard English allows two negatives only if a positive meaning is intended: The runners were *not unhappy* with their performance. Double negatives used to emphasize negation are nonstandard: Jack *doesn't* have to answer to *anybody* [not *nobody*].

due to   *Due to* is an adjective phrase and should not be used as a preposition meaning "because of": The trip was canceled *because of* [not *due to*] lack of interest. *Due to* is acceptable as a subject complement and usually follows a form of the verb *be*: His success *was due to* hard work.

effect   See *affect, effect*.

e.g.   Use *for example* or *for instance* in formal writing.

enthused   As an adjective, *enthusiastic* is preferred: The children were *enthusiastic* [not *enthused*] about going to the circus.

etc.   Avoid ending a list with *etc*. It is more emphatic to end with an example, and in most contexts readers will understand that the list is not exhaustive. When you don't wish to end with an example, *and so on* is more graceful than *etc.*

everyone, every one   *Everyone* is an indefinite pronoun: *Everyone* wanted to go. *Every one*, the pronoun *one* preceded by the adjective *every*, means "each individual or thing in a particular group." *Every one* is usually followed by *of*: *Every one of* the missing books was found.

except See *accept, except.*

farther, further *Farther* describes distances: Detroit is *farther* from Miami than I thought. *Further* suggests quantity or degree: You extended the curfew *further* than you should have.

fewer, less *Fewer* refers to items that can be counted; *less* refers to general amounts: *Fewer* people are living in the city. Please put *less sugar in my tea.*

further See *farther, further.*

good, well *Good* is an adjective, *well* an adverb: He hasn't felt *good* about his game since he sprained his wrist last season. She performed *well* on the uneven parallel bars. (See section 13.)

hanged, hung *Hanged* is the past-tense and past-participle form of the verb *hang*, meaning "to execute": The prisoner was *hanged* at dawn. *Hung* is the past-tense and past-participle form of the verb *hang*, meaning "to fasten or suspend": The stockings were *hung* by the chimney with care.

hardly Avoid expressions such as *can't hardly* and *not hardly*, which are considered double negatives: I *can* [not *can't*] hardly describe my elation at getting the job.

he At one time *he* was used to mean "he or she." Today such usage is inappropriate. See page 15 for alternative constructions.

hisself *Hisself* is nonstandard. Use *himself.*

hopefully *Hopefully* means "in a hopeful manner": We looked *hopefully* to the future. Do not use *hopefully* in constructions such as the following: *Hopefully*, your daughter will recover soon. Indicate who is doing the hoping: *I hope* that your daughter will recover soon.

hung See *hanged, hung.*

i.e. Use *that is* in formal writing.

illusion See *allusion, illusion.*

imply, infer *Imply* means "to suggest or state indirectly"; *infer* means "to draw a conclusion": John *implied* that he knew all about computers, but the interviewer *inferred* that John was inexperienced.

in regards to *In regards to* confuses two different phrases: *in regard to* and *as regards.* Use one or the other: *In regard to* [or *As regards*] the contract, ignore the first clause.

irregardless   *Irregardless* is nonstandard. Use *regardless*.

is when, is where   These mixed constructions are often incorrectly used in definitions: A run-off election *is a second election held to break a tie* [not *is when a second election is held to break a tie*].

it is   *It is* is nonstandard when used to mean "there is": *There is* [not *It is*] a fly in my soup.

its, it's   *Its* is a possessive pronoun; *it's* is a contraction for *it is*: The dog licked *its* wound whenever *its* owner walked into the room. *It's* a perfect day to walk the twenty-mile trail.

kind of, sort of   Avoid using *kind of* or *sort of* to mean "somewhat": The movie was *a little* [not *kind of*] boring. Do not put *a* after either phrase: That *kind of* [not *kind of a*] salesclerk annoys me.

lead, led   *Lead* is a noun referring to a metal. *Led* is the past tense of the verb *to lead*: He *led* me to the treasure.

learn, teach   *Learn* means "to gain knowledge"; *teach* means "to impart knowledge": I must *teach* [not *learn*] my sister to read.

leave, let   Avoid the nonstandard use of *leave* ("to exit") to mean *let* ("to permit"): *Let* [not *Leave*] me help you with the dishes.

less   See *fewer, less*.

let, leave   See *leave, let.*

liable   *Liable* means "obligated" or "responsible." Do not use it to mean "likely": You're *likely* [not *liable*] to trip if you don't tie your shoelaces.

lie, lay   *Lie* is an intransitive verb meaning "to recline or rest on a surface." Its forms are *lie, lies, lay, lain,* and *lying. Lay* is a transitive verb meaning "to put or place." Its forms are *lay, lays, laid, laid,* and *laying.* (See pp. 21–23.)

like, as   *Like* is a preposition, not a subordinating conjunction. It should be followed only by a noun or a noun phrase. *As* is a subordinating conjunction that introduces a subordinate clause. In casual speech you may say *She looks like she hasn't slept* or *You don't know her like I do.* But in formal writing, use *as*: She looks *as if* she hasn't slept. You don't know her *as* I do.

loose, lose   *Loose* is an adjective meaning "not securely fastened." *Lose* is a verb meaning "to misplace" or "to not win": Did you *lose* your only *loose* pair of work pants?

may See *can, may*.

maybe, may be *Maybe* is an adverb meaning "possibly"; *may be* is a verb phrase: *Maybe* the sun will shine tomorrow. Tomorrow *may be* a brighter day.

may of, might of *May of* and *might of* are nonstandard for *may have* and *might have*.

media, medium *Media* is the plural of *medium*: Of all the *media* that cover the Olympics, television is the *medium* that best captures the spectacle of the events.

most Avoid *most* to mean "almost": *Almost* [not *Most*] everyone went to the parade.

must of See *may of*.

myself *Myself* is a reflexive or intensive pronoun. Reflexive: I cut *myself*. Intensive: I will drive you *myself*. Do not use *myself* in place of *I* or *me*: He gave the plants to Melinda and *me* [not *myself*].

nowheres *Nowheres* is nonstandard for *nowhere*.

number See *amount, number*.

of Use the verb *have*, not the preposition *of*, after the verbs *could, should, would, may, might,* and *must*: They *must have* [not *must of*] left early.

off of *Off* is sufficient. Omit *of*.

passed, past *Passed* is the past tense of the verb *to pass*: Emily *passed* me another slice of cake. *Past* usually means "belonging to a former time" or "beyond a time or place": Our *past* president spoke until *past* midnight. The hotel is just *past* the next intersection.

plus *Plus* should not be used to join independent clauses: This raincoat is dirty; *moreover* [not *plus*], it has a hole in it.

precede, proceed *Precede* means "to come before." *Proceed* means "to go forward": As we *proceeded* up the mountain, we noticed fresh tracks in the mud, evidence that a group of hikers had *preceded* us.

principal, principle *Principal* is a noun meaning "the head of a school or organization" or "a sum of money." It is also an adjective meaning "most important." *Principle* is a noun meaning "a basic truth or law": The *principal* expelled her for three *principal* reasons. We believe in the *principle* of equal justice for all.

proceed, precede See *precede, proceed*.

quote, quotation   *Quote* is a verb; *quotation* is a noun. Avoid
using *quote* as a shortened form of the noun: Her *quotations*
[not *quotes*] from Shakespeare intrigued us.

real, really   *Real* is an adjective; *really* is an adverb. *Real* is
sometimes used informally as an adverb, but avoid this use
in formal writing: She was *really* [not real] angry. (See section
13.)

reason is because   Use *that* instead of *because*: The *reason*
I'm late *is that* [not *is because*] my car broke down.

reason why   The expression *reason why* is redundant: *The*
reason [not *The reason why*] Jones lost the election is clear.

respectfully, respectively   *Respectfully* means "showing or
marked by respect": He *respectfully* submitted his opinion to
the judge. *Respectively* means "each in the order given: John,
Tom, and Larry were a butcher, a baker, and a lawyer, *re-*
spectively.

sensual, sensuous   *Sensual* means "gratifying the physical
senses," especially those associated with sexual pleasure.
Sensuous means "pleasing to the senses," especially those
involved in the experience of art, music, and nature: The *sen-*
suous music and balmy air led the dancers to more *sensual*
movements.

set, sit   *Set* means "to put" or "to place"; *sit* means "to be
seated": She *set* the dough in a warm corner of the kitchen.
The cat sits in the warmest part of the room.

should of   *Should of* is nonstandard for *should have*.

since   Do not use *since* to mean "because" if there is any
chance of ambiguity: *Because* [not *Since*] we won the game,
we have been celebrating with a pitcher of beer. *Since* here
could mean "because" or "from the time that."

sit   See *set, sit*.

site, cite   See *cite, site*.

sure and   *Sure and* is nonstandard for *sure to*.

take   See *bring, take*.

than, then   *Than* is a conjunction used in comparisons; *then*
is an adverb denoting time: That pizza is more *than* I can eat.
Tom laughed, and *then* we recognized him.

that   See *who, which, that*.

that, which   Many writers reserve *that* for restrictive clauses,
which for nonrestrictive clauses. (See p. 51.)

theirselves   *Theirselves* is nonstandard for *themselves*.

them   The use of *them* in place of *those* is nonstandard: Please send *those* [not *them*] letters to the sponsors.

there, their, they're   *There* is an adverb specifying place; it is also an expletive. Adverb: Sylvia is lying *there* unconscious. Expletive: *There* are two plums left. *Their* is a possessive pronoun: Fred and Jane finally washed *their* car. *They're* is a contraction of *they are*: Surprisingly, *they're* late today.

they   The use of *they* to indicate possession is nonstandard. Use *their* instead: Cindy and Sam decided to sell *their* [not *they*] boat.

to, too, two   *To* is a preposition; *too* is an adverb; *two* is a number: *Too* many of your shots slice *to* the left, but the last *two* were right on the mark.

toward, towards   *Toward* and *towards* are generally interchangeable, although *toward* is preferred.

try and   *Try and* is nonstandard for *try to*.

unique   Avoid expressions such as *most unique*, *more straight*, *less perfect*, *very round*. It is illogical to suggest degrees of such absolute concepts as *unique*.

use to, suppose to   *Use to* and *suppose* to are nonstandard for *used to* and *supposed to*.

wait for, wait on   *Wait for* means "to be in readiness for" or "await." *Wait on* means "to serve": We're only *waiting for* [not *waiting on*] Ruth before we can leave.

ways   *Ways* is colloquial when used to mean "distance": The city is a long *way* [not *ways*] from here.

weather, whether   The noun *weather* refers to the state of the atmosphere. *Whether* is a conjunction referring to a choice between alternatives: We wondered *whether* the *weather* would clear up in time for our picnic.

where   Do not use *where* in place of *that*: I heard *that* [not *where*] the crime rate is increasing.

which   See *that, which* and *who, which, that*.

while   Avoid using *while* to mean "although" or "whereas" if there is any chance of ambiguity: *Although* [not *While*] Gloria lost money in the slot machine, Tom won it at roulette. Here *While* could mean either "although" or "at the same time that."

who, which, that   Use *who*, not *which*, to refer to persons. Generally, use *that* to refer to things or, occasionally, to a group or class of people: Fans wondered how an old *man who* [*not that* or *which*] walked with a limp could play football. The *team that* scores the most points in this game will win the tournament.

who, whom   *Who* is used for subjects and subject complements; *whom* is used for objects. (See pp. 33–34.)

who's, whose   Who's is a contraction of *who is*; *whose* is a possessive pronoun: *Who's* ready for more popcorn? *Whose* coat is this?

would of   *Would of* is nonstandard for *would have*.

you   In formal writing, avoid *you* in an indefinite sense meaning "anyone": *Any spectator* [not *You*] could tell by the way John caught the ball that his throw would be too late. (See pp. 30–31.)

your, you're   *Your* is a possessive pronoun; *you're* is a contraction of *you are*: Is that *your* new motorcycle? *You're* on the list of finalists.

32. Glossary of grammatical terms

This glossary gives definitions for parts of speech, such as nouns; parts of sentences, such as subjects; and types of sentences, clauses, and phrases.

If you are looking up the name of an error (sentence fragment, for example), consult the index or the table of contents instead.

absolute phrase   A word group that modifies a whole clause or sentence, usually consisting of a noun followed by a participle or participial phrase: *His tone suggesting no hint of humor*, the minister told us to love our enemies because it would drive them nuts.

active vs. passive voice   When a verb is in the active voice, the subject of the sentence does the action: The early *bird catches* the early worm. In the passive voice, the subject receives the action: The early *worm is* sometimes *caught* by the early bird. Often the actor does not appear in the passive-voice sentence: The early *worm is* sometimes *caught*. (See also pp. 3–5 and 26–27.)

adjective   A word used to modify (describe) a noun or pronoun: the *lame* dog, *rare old* stamps, *sixteen* candles. Adjectives usually answer one of these questions: Which one? What kind of? How many or how much? (See also pp. 34–36.)

adjective clause   A subordinate clause that modifies a noun or pronoun. An adjective clause begins with a relative pronoun (*who, whom, whose, which, that*) or a relative adverb (*when, where*) and usually appears right after the word it modifies: The arrow *that has left the bow* never returns.

adverb   A word used to modify a verb, an adjective, or another adverb: rides *smoothly, unusually* attractive, *very* slowly. An adverb usually answers one of these questions: When? Where? How? Why? Under what conditions? To what degree? (See also pp. 34–35.)

adverb clause   A subordinate clause that modifies a verb (or occasionally an adjective or adverb). An adverb clause begins with a subordinating conjunction such as *although, because, if, unless,* or *when* and usually appears at the beginning or the end of a sentence: *When the well is dry*, we know the worth of water. Don't talk *unless you can improve the silence.*

agreement   See pages 17–21 and 27–29.

antecedent   A noun or pronoun to which a pronoun refers: When the *wheel* squeaks, *it* is greased. *Wheel* is the antecedent of the pronoun *it.*

appositive   A noun or noun phrase that renames a nearby noun or pronoun: Politicians, *acrobats at heart,* can lean on both sides of an issue at once.

article   The word *a, an, the,* used to mark a noun. (See also pp. 41–43.)

case   See pages 31–34.

clause   A word group containing a subject, a verb, and any objects, complements, or modifiers of the verb. See *independent clause, subordinate clause.*

complement   See *subject complement, object complement.*

complex sentence   A sentence consisting of one independent clause and one or more subordinate clauses. In the following example, the subordinate clause is italicized: Do not insult the mother alligator *until you have crossed the river.*

compound sentence   A sentence consisting of two independent clauses. The clauses are usually joined by a comma and a coordinating conjunction (*and, but, or, nor, for, so, yet*) or by a semicolon: One arrow is easily broken, but you can't break a bundle of ten. Love is blind; envy has its eyes wide open.

compound-complex sentence   A sentence consisting of at least two independent clauses and at least one subordinate clause. In the following example, the subordinate clauses are italicized: Tell me *what you eat*, and I will tell you *what you are*.

conjunction   A joining word. See *coordinating conjunction, correlative conjunction, subordinating conjunction, conjunctive adverb*.

conjunctive adverb   An adverb used with a semicolon to connect independent clauses: If an animal does something, we call it instinct; *however*, if we do the same thing, we call it intelligence. The most commonly used conjunctive adverbs are *consequently, furthermore, however, moreover, nevertheless, then, therefore*, and *thus*. See page 57 for a more complete list.

coordinating conjunction   One of the following words, used to join elements of equal grammatical rank: *and, but, or, nor, for, so, yet.*

correlative conjunction   A pair of conjunctions connecting grammatically equal elements: *either . . . or, neither . . . nor, whether . . . or, not only . . . but also*, and *both . . . and.*

demonstrative pronoun   A pronoun used to identify or point to a noun: *this, that, these, those. This* hanging will surely be a lesson to me.

direct object   A word or word group that receives the action of the verb: The little snake studies *the ways of the big serpent*. The complete direct object is *the ways of the big serpent*. The simple direct object is always a noun or pronoun, such as *ways*.

expletive   The word *there* or *it* when used at the beginning of a sentence to delay the subject: *There* are many paths to the top of the mountain. *It* is not good to wake a sleeping lion. The delayed subjects are the noun *paths* and the infinitive phrase *to wake a sleeping lion*.

gerund   A verb form ending in *-ing*, used as a noun: Continual *dripping* wears away a stone. *Dripping* is used as the subject of the verb *wears away*.

gerund phrase   A gerund and its objects, complements, or modifiers. A gerund phrase always functions as a noun, usually as a subject, a subject complement, or a direct object. In the following example, the phrase functions as a subject: *Justifying a fault* doubles it.

helping verb   One of the following words, when used with a main verb: *be, am, is, are, was, were, being, been; has, have, had; do, does, did; can, will, shall, should, could, would, may, might, must.* Helping verbs always precede main verbs: *will work, is working, had worked.*

indefinite pronoun   A pronoun that refers to a nonspecific person or thing: *Anyone* who serves God for money will serve the Devil for better wages. The most common indefinite pronouns are *all, another, any, anybody, anyone, anything, both, each, either, everybody, everyone, everything, few, many, neither, nobody, none, no one, nothing, one, some, somebody, someone, something.*

independent clause   A clause that stands alone as a sentence or that could stand alone. See also *clause.*

indirect object   A noun or pronoun that names to whom or for whom the action is done: Fate gives *us* our relatives. An indirect object always precedes a direct object, in this case *our relatives.*

infinitive   The word *to* followed by a verb: *to think, to dream.*

infinitive phrase   An infinitive and its objects, complements, or modifiers. An infinitive phrase can function as a noun, an adjective, or an adverb: *To side with truth* is noble. We do not have the right *to abandon the poor.* Do not use a hatchet *to remove a fly from your friend's forehead.*

intensive or reflexive pronoun   A pronoun ending in *-self*: *myself, yourself, himself, herself, itself, ourselves, yourselves, themselves.* An intensive pronoun emphasizes a noun or another pronoun: I *myself* don't understand my moods. A reflexive pronoun names a receiver of an action identical with the doer of the action: Did you cut *yourself*?

interjection   A word expressing surprise or emotion: *Oh! Wow! Hey! Hooray!*

interrogative pronoun   A pronoun used to open a question: *who, whom, whose, which, what. What* does history teach us?

intransitive verb   See *transitive and intransitive verbs.*

irregular verb   See *regular and irregular verbs.* Or see pages 21–24.

linking verb   A verb that links a subject to a subject complement, a word or word group that renames or describes the subject: Prejudice *is* the child of ignorance. Good medicine sometimes *tastes* bitter. The most common linking verbs are forms of *be*: *be, am, is, are, was, were, being, been.* The following verbs sometimes function as linking verbs: *appear, become, feel, grow, look, make, seem, smell, sound, taste.*

modifier   A word, phrase, or clause that describes or qualifies the meaning of a word. Modifiers include adjectives, adverbs, prepositional phrases, participial phrases, some infinitive phrases, and adjective and adverb clauses.

mood   See page 26.

noun   The name of a person, place, or thing: The *cat* in *gloves* catches no *mice.* Nouns are classified for a variety of purposes. When capitalization is the issue, we speak of *proper* versus *common* nouns (see pp. 70–71). If the problem involves the use of articles, we distinguish between *count* nouns and *non-count* nouns (see pp. 41–43). Most nouns come in *singular* or *plural* forms; *collective nouns* may be either singular or plural (see pp. 19 and 29). *Possessive* nouns require an apostrophe (see pp. 59–60).

noun clause   A subordinate clause that functions as a noun, usually as a subject, a subject complement, or a direct object. In the following sentence, the italicized noun clauses function as subject and subject complement: *What history teaches us* is *that we have never learned anything from it.* Noun clauses usually begin with *how, who, whom, that, what, whether,* or *why.*

noun equivalent   A word or word group that functions like a noun: a pronoun, a noun and its modifiers, a gerund phrase, some infinitive phrases, a noun clause.

object   See *direct object, indirect object.*

object complement   A word or word group that renames or describes a direct object. It always appears after the direct object: Our fears do make us *traitors.* Love makes all hard hearts *gentle.*

object of a preposition   See *prepositional phrase.*

participial phrase   A present or past participle and its objects, complements, or modifiers. A participial phrase always functions as an adjective, to describe a noun or pronoun. Usually it appears before or after the word it modifies: *Being weak,* foxes are distinguished by superior tact. Truth *kept in the dark* will never save the world.

participle, past   A verb form usually ending in *-d, -ed, -n, -en,* or *-t: asked, spoken, stolen.* Although past participles usually function as main verbs (*was asked, had spoken*), they may also be used as adjectives (the *stolen* car).

participle, present   A verb form ending in *-ing*. Although present participles usually function as main verbs (*is rising*), they may also be used as adjectives (the *rising* tide).

parts of speech   A system for classifying words. Many words can function as more than one part of speech. See *noun, pronoun, verb, adjective, adverb, preposition, conjunction, interjection*.

passive voice   See *active vs. passive voice*.

personal pronoun   One of the following pronouns, used to refer to a specific person or thing: *I, me, you, she, her, he, him, it. Admonish your friends in private; praise *them* in public.

phrase   A word group that lacks a subject, a verb, or both. Most phrases function within sentences as adjectives, as adverbs, or as nouns. See *absolute phrase, appositive phrase, gerund phrase, infinitive phrase, participial phrase, prepositional phrase*.

possessive case   See page 31.

possessive pronoun   A pronoun used to indicate ownership: *my, mine, your, yours, her, hers, his, its, our, ours, your, yours, their, theirs*. A cock has great influence on *his* own dunghill.

predicate   A verb and any objects, complements, and modifiers that go with it: A clean glove *often hides a dirty hand*.

preposition   A word placed before a noun or noun equivalent to form a phrase modifying another word in the sentence. The preposition indicates the relation between the noun (or noun equivalent) and the word the phrase modifies. The most common prepositions are *about, above, across, after, against, along, among, around, at, before, behind, below, beside, besides, between, beyond, by, down, during, except, for, from, in, inside, into, like, near, next, of, off, on, onto, out, outside, over, past, since, than, through, to, toward, under, unlike, until, up, with*, and *without*.

prepositional phrase   A prepositional phrase begins with a preposition and ends with a noun or noun equivalent (called the object of the preposition). Most prepositional phrases function as adjectives or adverbs. Adjective phrases usually come right after the noun or pronoun they modify: Variety is the spice *of life*. Adverb phrases usually appear at the beginning or the end of the sentence: *To the ant*, a few drops of rain are a flood. Do not judge a tree *by its bark*.

progressive verb forms   See pages 24–25.

pronoun   A word used for a noun. Usually the pronoun substitutes for a specific noun, known as its antecedent. In the following example, *elephant* is the antecedent of the pronoun *him*: When an *elephant* is in trouble, even a frog will kick *him*. See also *demonstrative pronoun*, *indefinite pronoun*, *intensive or reflexive pronoun*, *interrogative pronoun*, *personal pronoun*, *possessive pronoun*, *relative pronoun*.

regular and irregular verbs   When a verb is regular, both the past tense and past participle are formed by adding *-ed* or *-d* to the dictionary form of the word: *walk*, *walked*, *walked*. Irregular verbs are formed in a variety of other ways: *ride*, *rode*, *ridden*; *begin*, *began*, *begun*; *go*, *went*, *gone*; and so on. See also pages 21–24.

relative adverb   The word *when* or *where*, when used to introduce an adjective clause.

relative pronoun   One of the following words, when used to introduce an adjective clause: *who*, *whom*, *whose*, *which*, *that*. A fable is a bridge *that* leads to truth.

sentence   A word group consisting of at least one independent clause. See also *simple sentence*, *compound sentence*, *complex sentence*, *compound-complex sentence*.

simple sentence   A sentence consisting of one independent clause and no subordinate clauses: The frog in the well knows nothing of the ocean.

subject   A word or word group that names who or what the sentence is about. In the following example, the complete subject (the simple subject and all of its modifiers) is italicized: *Historical books that contain no lies* are tedious. The simple subject is *books*. See also *subject after verb*, *understood subject*.

subject after verb   Although the subject normally precedes the verb, sentences are sometimes inverted. In the following example, the subject *the real tinsel* comes after the verb *lies*: Behind the phony tinsel of Hollywood lies *the real tinsel*. When a sentence begins with the expletive *there* or *it*, the subject always follows the verb. See *expletive*.

subject complement   A word or word group that follows a linking verb and either renames or describes the subject of the sentence. If the subject complement renames the subject, it is a noun or a noun equivalent: The handwriting on the wall may be *a forgery*. If it describes the subject, it is an adjective: Love is *blind*.

subjunctive mood See page 26.

subordinate clause A clause that cannot stand alone as a sentence. Subordinate clauses function within sentences as adjectives, adverbs, or nouns. See *adjective clause*, *adverb clause*, *noun clause*.

subordinating conjunction A word that introduces a subordinate clause and indicates its relation to the rest of the sentence. The most common subordinating conjunctions are *after*, *although*, *as*, *as if*, *because*, *before*, *even though*, *if*, *since*, *so that*, *than*, *that*, *though*, *unless*, *until*, *when*, *where*, *whether*, and *while*. Note: The relative pronouns *who*, *whom*, *whose*, *which*, and *that* also introduce subordinate clauses.

tenses See pages 24–26.

transitive and intransitive verbs Transitive verbs take direct objects, nouns or noun equivalents that receive the action. In the following example, the transitive verb *loves* takes the direct object *its mother*: A spoiled child never *loves* its mother. Intransitive verbs do not take direct objects: Money *talks*. If any words follow an intransitive verb, they are adverbs or word groups functioning as adverbs: The sun *will set* without your assistance.

understood subject The subject *you* when it is understood but not actually present in the sentence. Understood subjects occur in sentences that issue commands or advice: [You] Hitch your wagon to a star.

verb A word that expresses action (*jump*, *think*) or being (*is*, *was*). A sentence's verb is composed of a main verb possibly preceded by one or more helping verbs: The best fish *swim* near the bottom. A marriage *is* not *built* in a day. Verbs have five forms: the dictionary form (*walk*, *ride*), the *-s* form (*walks*, *rides*), the past-tense form (*walked*, *rode*), the past participle (*walked*, *ridden*), and the present principle (*walking*, *riding*).

verbal phrase See *gerund phrase*, *infinitive phrase*, *participial phrase*.

Index

Contents